For Yvonne, my family and past pupils.

Reviews for Mr Mac.

A unique account of a teaching life, which concentrates on the practice and not the theory. This is an honest, engaging and insightful book, which reveals much about the humanity that drives our education system. Devoid of sentimentality and self-congratulation, it skilfully encapsulates the hard work, mischievousness, eccentricity, humour and commitment to an all-rounded education that makes a teacher of distinction. This is the story of an educator willing to learn from mistakes and savour the triumphs, while revealing that for the truly committed teacher, a life in the classroom is as much about learning lessons as teaching them.

Diarmaid Ferriter.
Professor of Modern Irish History at University College Dublin.
18th November 2009

This book is shot through with that strange mixture of humility and ego which great teachers have, that knowledge that every day in front of the blackboard is a performance, delivered in the service of others. Every Government minister should read Mr Mac because in a world where education, health and sport are being pillaged doing things for the sheer love of doing them, for the intrinsic value and fulfilment that they offer, might be a way forward.

Tom Humphries.
Irish Times 28th December 2009.

The late Bryan MacMahon, teacher and author, once described a good teacher as "a good person, teaching". In this book, Maurice McMahon provides a wonderful insight into his lifetime in the classroom with pupils whom he regarded as the 'source of his life and energy'. Mr Mac should be read by anybody who regards teaching as 'special work that always has to be approached with reverence'. His great love of the teaching/learning experience comes across throughout and it is clear that Maurice excited, inspired and engaged his pupils in his classroom work. This book is the story of a committed learner who constantly developed his own practice as a teacher throughout his many years in the classroom.

Eamon Stack. Chief Inspector (1997-2009).
Department of Education & Science, Ireland.

Maurice McMahon taught me in St. Michael's, Listowel from 1966-1968 and he demonstrates in this welcome memoir, he was and continues to be throughout his teaching career enthusiastic, insightful, honest, strict yet friendly, traditional yet subversive. Like all great teachers he has the gift of seeing himself as other see him. Mr Mac sits on my bookshelf, a worthy companion to The Master.

Gabriel Fitzmaurice.
File & Údar. Moyvane.

Copyright Maurice McMahon 2009

Cover image copyright
© David Freund / iStockPhoto

ISBN 0-9551115-5-2

Reprinted May 2010
First published November 2009

'Mr. Mac' - A Blackboard Memoir

Written by;
Maurice McMahon.
Available only from mrmacbenildus@gmail.com

FOREWORD

"I bet you have some stories to tell." This was the brief comment uttered by a parent of a former pupil in the Airport queue as we boarded a return flight from Tenerife shortly after I retired from teaching. Baffled at first with our chance meeting, confused also by my new bushy beard, fishing in the air for a name he finally spluttered ... "Benildus! Macker! I hear you cashed in your chips," adding with a wry smile, "I bet you have some stories to tell." The new life that awaited me I had decided deserved a new image, hence the beard, trusting if only jokingly that it might bring anonymity and security from the legions of pupils whose lives, some might say, I lorded over and dominated, but yet hopefully influenced perhaps over a career of forty years teaching.

I thanked him for his good wishes, took my window seat and thought little of his throw away remark. However, during the four-hour flight home the comment surfaced and created an itch until I convinced myself that I might indeed have a worthwhile tale to tell. There and then, high in the sky the floodgates of memory were thrown open. By touchdown I had jotted down the chapter headings on the in-flight magazine, covering a life spent in classrooms, dedicated to instruction. The worst pencil they say is better than a bad memory. I operated in an arena, a classroom, far from the beating heart of power but close to the beating heart of adolescents.

Now that the curtain has been drawn and I exit the stage, it is on a personal level vitally important that the cacophony and pandemonium of voices, faces and incidents of countless pupils forever young who still people my skull, some that haunt and bombard daily, be finally expelled and ejected, for better or for worse, as they now occupy valuable space in an ever diminishing memory bank. Call this an eviction, even a spring cleaning at this late stage if you so desire; all I am sure of is that for sanity sake it must be undertaken before any future is faced.

Whether the story to be told deserves telling is open for debate. It may be of passing interest to some ageing former student that their old teacher always had a deep desire and wish to make himself known and understood more fully to them, as the impressions formed of teachers by pupils in their formative years are partial and incomplete.

Many people attempt to log and give meaning, though not all on paper, to their own personal journey in life. The classroom and the pupils were always the centre of my adult world, the source of my life and energy. They drove me forward and helped me to know myself and understand my own psyche. Teaching was special work that always had to be approached with reverence. Now that those days are over, I would like to think that I made a positive contribution. Any recollections are at best a plea for understanding. Like a clockmaker, I am eager to demonstrate the inner workings of the teaching process. In this memoir I wish to share the intimacy, excitement, tension, and glorious unpredictability of the daily classroom. How effective any educator is, and what was achieved within the confines of my classroom, is for others to decide.

I was fortunate to have been involved in the very early setting up of a college in a semi -rural landscape in the late sixties before it became part of the widening suburbia of south Dublin. Year after year I witnessed the slow burning urbanisation, brick on brick that changed totally the view from the upstairs school windows of the patchwork quilt of fields I first looked out on as a young teacher.

Above all I wish to thank and pay deserved tribute to all those pupils I taught and who gave me in return much more than they ever realised. To repeat an often-used expression in class, imagine being paid to enjoy standing at a blackboard and talking for a living!

And yet in spite of our daily contact, my life after school was a mystery to these same individuals. This never ceased to amuse me. I inhabited their world, but never they mine. If this was the reality of city life, it was no less artificial. As a countryman in the city it indicated an absence of rootedness. My obsessions, passions, family and home life went unknown. In my Kerry youth in a small country town the teacher's life and mine were intertwined daily, in and out of the class-room. It helped me to make allowances, be more understanding, even forgiving at times in my overall assessment of those masters and ped-agogues who dominated my teenage years. Back then I had the full picture and never had to judge solely from the standard teacher's mask donned for the classroom. My own pupils in the relative anonymity of Dublin were obviously denied this opportunity.

Did they now in turn view me as an authority figure, a cardboard giant, one dimensional, and at best functional? I was privy to their world through communicating and meeting with parents, but that alas was a one-way route of information. I can still see the surprise and shock reaction of one 17 year old when I informed him that I had 4 teenage children of my own. From that day forth he, I believe, began to look at me in a different light and softened also in his approach. Maybe it was sympathy for my children that I observed! In this story I hope to flesh out the picture, however belatedly.

I always placed a high importance on the sanctity of the individuals I taught; it was a privilege to dance and prance in their company and treat each as if he were a family member. The memories that remain are a priceless treasure that would sustain me on any desert island. Bidding adieu was never easy. Retired now I consider the efforts made and assistance given to pupils was no more than duty called for. Such is the way of the world, as an extended family, they flew when they fledged.

Not everybody is afforded the glorious opportunity of working in an occupation that they love. I was one of the lucky ones, happy and ful-filled, fortunate in the extreme. I classify those I met and taught as friends; I bear no grudges and can look them and life straight in the eye, safe in the knowledge that I had given my all. I now scan the fu-ture horizons and the challenges left to me outside of teaching, but not before inviting whoever so wishes, known or unknown to me, to fall into step and cross a school threshold again.

THE LAST HURRAH

My last day in school, after thirty-nine years teaching, passed by unnoticed. There was no Last Day, simply a 'Last Hurrah' night class months later – an event that needs clarification and explanation. What took place on the occasion over a two-hour period was in all humility a 'Field of Dreams' type experience that few are privileged to experience. On a personal level this last minute diversionary tactic turned out to be a night of all nights to be savoured and recalled in the more sedate atmosphere of retirement. In that never to be forgotten two-hour class session, the years rolled back as various former pupils trickled in. As names were announced, shy heads craned themselves around the partially opened door, some still harbouring moments of terror before deciding to enter for one last time the close confines of the caged room, known only too well by all, there to find their old teacher still standing tall and cracking his whip. The recalled names and images of once energetic teenagers frozen and imprinted on my brain now bore little resemblance to those who, one by one, timidly tip-toed instinctively to favoured positions they had occupied in the past. Balding, bearded and bellied middle-aged men now squeezed themselves into the groaning desks. Soon standing room was at a premium. Thankfully, and somehow inexplicably, the once familiar voices like echoes were recalled, they had changed little, they still rang true and key-like, instantly unlocked the memory bank. The hard disk drive was booted and shocked into dredging up filed away information from a distant era.

All very civilized and friendly at first, as many I had not seen for over thirty years trickled in slowly. But when the floodwaters burst, torrents of abuse, laughter, accusations, and ribald comments, wave-like crashed, exploded and echoed in the confined room over those two short hours. It was old times recaptured. I was young again, 'in my prime', like the hero of the silver screen. This indeed was the madness of Mr. Sermon in Delderfield's novel. Thankfully none of the school authorities or senior staff were present. Had they been, faces other than mine would have blushed. For the first time in my life I understood the full import of the expression 'winging it'.

Throwing caution to the wind in the banter, question time and arguments that followed, I gave as good as I got. Somehow I went the full fifteen rounds, slightly bruised as old times and stories were recalled. Past indiscretions even secrets, were dredged up on both sides and aired openly.

'What about the public flogging, Sir, in the yard long ago? The apple-throwing incident, the boy from Ranelagh, six o' the best, public execution. He was only half guilty. You over-reacted.'

'And what about the anonymous letter you received, that letter to the culchie, did you ever find out who wrote it? You had somebody down for it, did he ever admit it? Were you insulted?'

'What was all that carry-on in class about being an expert in hand-writing, saying you worked as a Detective in Dublin Castle before you took up teaching and that you were a forensic scientist? Did you-know-who, ever own up?'

As a latter day Don Quixote I mounted my trusty steed and rode out, battling and repulsing foes on all fronts in the crowded confines of that small classroom. Nobody was spared in the heat of battle as old scores had finally to be settled. No quarter was given or asked for. Speak now, I advised them, as this was to be the final settling of accounts. Those present did not hold back or spare me; they needed no prompting on this, their last opportunity. Believe me when I say that both sides availed of it. They took me at my word, if not apart. Rejuvenated as if by magic, a free spirit now, excited, enthused, intoxicated by their company I was back again a young inexperienced teacher flying free by the seat of my pants. This indeed was the freedom and nectar I had tasted of old, and in regret was now abandoning.

Cut to the chase. Tell them how it was on your last day, not your last night, I find myself echoing the long-standing advice given to pupils over the years. So what if I agree with or even copy the advice of Russian short story writers who compared stories to race horses. 'Get a good start, and progress from there.'

In contrast to that night, my last official day in school at the end of May 2005 was uneventful and simple, like so many others. Only the Principal and a few close colleagues/friends were aware of my intentions to call it a day. This was as I wished it and following the routine annual staff photograph at midday before the school broke up for the summer holidays, I walked unseen out the back door of the Woodwork Room, my refuge, and quietly if emotionally slinked away from a chosen career that had absorbed and consumed my best efforts. Inwardly I sighed with relief and satisfaction that I had been privileged to play some part in the education of a community nestled at the foothills of the Dublin Mountains.

With confidence I welcomed the approaching freedom and the challenge of new horizons. How often down the years had I promised myself that some day I would follow in the cycle tracks of the Tour De France and complete a stage in the French Pyrenees. Were these not the same mountains I would walk over in my long pilgrimage to Santiago? What of the long list of former pupils scattered across the globe that I had promised to look up? Their addresses had been carefully filed away and regularly updated. Had they not been forewarned in the long ago that when they least expected it a knock on their doors would find me, rucksack on my back, a pensioner, looking for a bed for the night in my trip around the world. Most pupils in fairness had extended such invitations; others in charity had said they would not see me stuck as long as it was for a single night only. Where my wife was going to fit into these dreams I never did quite work out.

The timing of my last day as a teacher, an important day in my life, was for the most part decided and dictated by matters of health and would not have been my preferred choice, as I always looked forward to going the full course of forty years plus at the blackboard if for no reason but to extract the full pension out of the Department. For far too long we gave them our life's blood, unappreciated and taken for granted as we were as teachers in society. 'Don't let them off the hook that easily. Live as long as you can and die when you can't,' was a phrase I subscribed to. Alas too soon, considerations of health counselled otherwise. The decision to retire early was a personal one after an extended period of sick leave, and now looking out and listening to the mid-Atlantic waves break and thunder on a Tenerife shore in early January, I certainly have no regrets. Are teachers one of the last of the professions destined to spend a lifetime in the same occupation if not in the same room? Can today's young working generation comprehend this life sentence of forty years or more? I doubt it. Time marches on relentlessly, one either falls into step or risks getting left behind, as many believe we did. When we were accused of only working half a day for half a week in half a year, I quickly added in defence, for half pay, with the promise of a pension to see me out.

Thirty years previously I had been present at my father's retirement as a local schoolmaster in a Kerry school where teaching was, and continues to be, part of our family tradition. Witnessing from the wings I vowed there and then that I would never submit myself to the ordeal of such a formal occasion as he had endured and certainly enjoyed on his last day in harness. His was a moving, emotional withdrawal organised for him in the local school hall at the end of day by appreciative parents and colleagues. A surprise send-off, the traditional one with of course half the parish in on the secret and present to play their part. A meaningful ceremony in a tightly knit community as they came to praise and pay tribute. If I recoiled instinctively from same, it was because of my temperament for which I make no apologies.

The whole occasion cum tribute I observed and tried to listen to objectively. In local terms, it was a great send-off. All the stops had been pulled out. As a gifted speaker and consummate actor my father revelled, even thrived, on such occasions, but the impact on me was so great that on leaving that packed auditorium, I vowed that I would never submit myself to such an emotional tsunami and ordeal. The ceremony formality, dressing up, presentations, false smiles and such occasions grated with me always. I view them as politicians do the rubber-chicken dinners between elections. Consequently when it came to my formal unannounced retirement, I recalled the past only too vividly and recoiled instinctively from this type of occasion, which I had in turn attended, deserved as they were, for many of my former colleagues.

This is the only explanation I offered for choosing to fold up my tent as I did, and like the Arabs, fade into the desert night across the sands of the approaching dunes. Never once did I look back, as in life I found that it is best to face into the wind and sing one's own song. I was happy then with this exit strategy, which eliminated stress, real or imagined, that any last day might bring. Incidentally I did not go home alone that day. Bicycle discarded, I kept my appointment with a senior pupil at the gate, as I exited the school grounds for the last time. To him and one other I had confided my departure having sworn them to secrecy days previously. Both had confidential, important matters on their minds with which I was helping and consequently I felt morally bound to keep them in the picture. At no stage did I want them to feel alone or let down with the issues they were struggling and agonising with across the following summer, now that I was walking out of their lives forever. They had my telephone number if help or advice was needed, even from a distance. Teenagers do not take kindly to false promises. As a favour to one, I accompanied him to Bray where we enquired about a possible Plasterer's apprenticeship. After two hours visiting building sites, with all loose ends tied up we both adjourned to my home where I bid my last scholar farewell. As he walked away and waved, I finally admitted to myself that I had really called it a day. Freedom beckoned.

But not just yet. My hackles rose. Some months later closed and locked doors were to be prised open again by the school authorities, much to my annoyance, in a request for a formal presentation at a time and place of my choosing. The cord that bound me to the school for years was still snagged and tugging. Was I never to be free, was the scene of old which I dreaded coming back to haunt me? My initial negative reply and refusal had to be reconsidered and it was only after serious consultation and advice and no small amount of convincing by close friends that I finally admitted that certain rubrics and formalities had to be observed in a civilised society. Finally I swallowed deeply and agreed to a formal farewell night.

Why did I relent? At worst a refusal could be open to serious misinterpretation, be impolite and give offence, even create an impression I certainly did not want to give. The compromise solution to my initial dilemma when finally forwarded was readily accepted by the college, which pleased me. My proposal, a two-fold one, was simple and instinctive, though considered bizarre at the time. In summary I asked that in any formal farewell night, speeches were to be severely curtailed, anything over three minutes, long winded, 'fadálach', any torrent of mushy and historically misleading sentimentality, deserved or otherwise, would see me bolt for the door. I was certainly laying down some ground rules, whether they were fully understood or not did not bother me too much. Sadly in the modern world, all too often the joys of brevity are succumbing to an epidemic of needless and often pointless speeches. I can silently hear my former pupils groan that I never practiced what I preached in this regard!

My second request, and more meaningful on a personal basis, was that this function be preceded by one last class strictly confined to past pupils, many of whom would I knew be on the wrong side of forty years of age. This request more than any thing else baffled the school authorities. If this was an unusual and novel request for them, to me it was the most natural and simple way to wind up a teaching career. There were to be no invitations issued; bush telegraph, word of mouth in the local area days previously would be sufficient for those who might be lucky enough to hear of such a class. In this way no offence was given or could be taken by any former student. The Vice Principal, himself a survivor of my classes, kindly undertook to spread the news that another one of their former tormentors was finally bowing out. This chosen format, unheard of at the time, would liberate me on the night from stress, pressure and the horrors of the type of occasion my father and many other teachers welcomed. It would simply be going through the motions of another class, granted that the age profile might be somewhat older. At least two former pupils, now teaching colleagues, could be relied upon to turn up for a chat in the designated classroom closest to the main door on the night agreed. Hopefully past pupils in the workforce on their way home might look in and linger before continuing with their busy evenings. These were the very people I felt most comfortable with, over a teaching life my real contract was with them. They knew me best or so they thought, warts and all.

11

I was forever conscious of my responsibilities to pupils and answerable at all times. Meeting them in odd places it was possible to look them in the eye and honestly account for my teaching stewardship. Open discussion was good for the soul; if I was to be found wanting, so be it. Any apologies due would be readily given. These chance callers would be a representative sample of those I shared my life with in good times, and bad.

There was no precedent for such a last farewell class and I could give the Principal no assurance or guidelines on anything in relation to the format, numbers etc. Then again, none were needed. One last class I knew would distract me from the brief formalities that were to follow. Under these conditions I was free from the dreaded hook that an imagination had suspended me on since my father's never forgotten fond adieu. I was in control of the situation, or at least that is what I thought.

How the sixty squashed people in that small classroom emerged without a physical blow struck on the night or a row starting, I will never understand. The spirit of the occasion can only be hinted at, certainly never fleshed out or recaptured. Now I fully understand the saying, 'Poetry is emotion recollected in tranquillity.' It was certainly poetry on the night that enriches itself when recalled later. No video camera was privy to events, at least I think not, but now in my saner moments I have a vague recollection of seeing the glimmer of a 'red eye' positioned on the windowsill. Was that a mini camera placed there? Technology left me behind years ago but if a copy does exist I appeal to the individual to please surface with it. I might even classify it as a historical family treasure! It was in truth an impromptu master class by all concerned. We were re-living a long lost dream. Had God called time on me there and then, I doubt if He could have chosen a more sublime occasion.

The past pupils, my audience, had been invited into the theatre of teaching, on to the stage. As an actor I revealed its inner most secrets, drew back the curtain in an effort to explain and expose temporarily the magic of the classroom with all its failures, frustrations and triumphs. Now with my worn mask discarded, the drama was finally over. I had allowed them glimpses of my other self, standing as it were naked, with no more secrets or magic box. The black thread bare gown, a theatrical prop of a lifetime seen and often feared by students lay cast aside in a limp, crumpled heap at my feet on the podium floor, a discarded shell that once had given me refuge. The show was over. The curtain came down slowly. Críoch. Finis. Terminado. I had come to the end of my teaching road.

I thanked them for their presence and patience, for the respect shown and honour paid. No greater tribute could have been given me. The friendship and loyalty of this representative group of past pupils was treasured. No outsiders viewed the performance. There had been no dress rehearsal; there would be no repeat performance. It was far from a one-man-show. There was no producer or director present on the night; if anything I was privileged to be one of the audience. They gave the performance of a lifetime and were deserving of my gratitude and respect and sustained applause. The impromptu script certainly left no room for mawkish sentimentality. My son who was entitled as a past pupil to be there was abroad. I regret his missing my finest hour. My daughters however did not qualify but I reminded myself that in my father's last day of teaching I had deposited my eldest, five years old, in his last official class where, seated among the pupils in an All Boys School she confounded the statement of a mother who the previous week had queried and stung my father by saying, "Forty five years, teaching boys? What? No girls? Sure you are only half a schoolmaster!" In my case there was no such accusation from any perceptive parent.

Only the persistent ringing of the bell outside in the October corridor called time on the 2-hour proceedings and broke the spell. Reluctantly and disorderly the raggle-taggle group adjourned to the location of the by now almost forgotten formal presentation. Raucous jibes, taunts, even applause accompanied the dead man walking down the long science corridor heralding a long-overdue arrival in the library where teachers and family awaited patiently.

Each pupil in his own way represented countless namesakes and absentees that I had the pleasure to teach and befriend. Suffice to say that in the Library the rubrics were observed. If not short, certainly sweet. The words of a dear past pupil, truthful or not, brought a suppressed tear to my eye.

"Shocked and stunned, Macker arrived into our lives like a Tasmanian Devil in 1968, all flowing robes, Kerry football shirt, with strict ideas of discipline and respect. There ensued a period of mental if not armed combat – we fought him in the classroom, we fought him in the yard, on the football pitch, and on the graffiti walls and desk-tops where the never-ending propaganda war of students vs teacher is often waged. The initial skirmishes lasted no more than three months and ended in a resounding – Draw! Because somehow, almost unbeknownst to us, we developed what initially was a begrudging respect for an adversary, but what very quickly became a sense of loyalty to, and shared common-purpose with, a leader and captor of minds. Soon we came to realise that, while he was tough (and he was!) he was also invariably fair, carrying many of us 'by the scruff of the neck' through examinations and he treated us with the same respect that he demanded from us. He spoke to us as adults, and he inspired us to find our own strengths and qualities, be they in books, hobbies or on the sports field. He looked out for the weak and the non-academics, and he celebrated and nurtured the talents of those in his care. With a never- failing interest in our education, development and welfare, after those few short years, he kept track of us in later life."

With these words I was left speechless and humbled. If the ground rules I had laid down for the night were not adhered to strictly those words penetrated and are still cherished. I have but one wish for those who retire and gave an honest effort over a lifetime, be it sufficient or not, that they too might enjoy and savour into old age an occasion such as I experienced on the night of my last hurrah.

A MOVE TO DUBLIN

If that was the end of my story, where did it begin? Following the traditional education in a small country town, at eighteen years of age
family finances allowed me follow my brothers to Dublin for further
education. Other classmates more deserving were denied this opportunity. I counted myself fortunate. The time spent at University in
Dublin between 1962 and 1966 while weird, wonderful and exciting,
was for me an uphill struggle on the academic front. The B.A.Degree
course at the time was considered, as it is now, a general preparation
for life particularly for those who wished to keep their options open
in the job market. In due course undecided about the future, I presented myself for enlightenment and polishing, but looking back from
today's vantage point I reluctantly admit that the benefits of the university experience somehow passed me by. Studying never came easy,
unstructured and unguided as my valiant efforts were, and the long
hours spent in study halls and public libraries were rarely as enjoyable
or rewarding as they should have been. Hard slog and determination
were a poor substitute for natural ability, but persevere I did, like a
bonded slave to the books.

There were times when better dividends might have been obtained
from praying rather than aimlessly studying. To compound the difficulties, career guidance was an unheard of commodity and the combined study of history and economics overloaded my system; either
on their own would have made more sense, as was the preferred option of most other B.A. candidates. It was too late in the day when this
fact finally dawned on me and changing horses mid stream did not
appeal to me at any juncture as it smacked of failure. Consequently it
came as no surprise when I found myself falling between two stools.
That, and the effort of writing up the cryptic notes of the then lecturer
and later Taoiseach, Dr.Garret Fitzgerald, could be likened to the squar-
ing of the circle. The fact that a landlady's daughter inadvertently
burnt a whole years lecture notes at a vital stage in the degree course
during a spring cleaning session did not help! Neither did a brief black-

out in my final examinations in the present day National Concert Hall, due to overstudy. For the first time in life the phrase 'looking into the abyss' was fully understood.

Admittedly the history studies were interesting and stimulating, but sadly where economics was concerned I might as well have been looking up a duck's arse, as a colleague so colourfully put it years later. Perseverance and doggedness finally paid off with an Honours Degree, not distinguished I add, which was gratefully accepted as an achievement in itself. Needless to say the Department of Finance together with the Whitaker programme for economic expansion managed successfully to drag Ireland out of the economic backwater of the late 50's without any assistance from such a qualified graduate!

It is difficult for any modern Irish student to grasp the reality of those dark days when the equivalent of a packed Croke Park emigrated annually. As one of the privileged few who had the opportunity of attending university there was never any danger of my wasting time or the hard earned money of parents with five boys, all of whom had third level ambitions. How they successfully managed to finance this in days before free education baffles me. It was only as parents in turn, that we the beneficiaries fully understood the sacrifices made by that generation. The time spent in university was a bitter experience that I gladly and quickly put behind me. Previous considerations of eventually going into business were quickly put on the back burner when information came that a teaching post was coming up in my old College in Kerry. If I drifted into teaching by accident, I would hate to think that the old cliché that 'those who can do, and those who can't, teach,' applied to me.

Digs or accommodation during those student days in various houses in Rathmines and Ranelagh was certainly a novelty and an education in itself for a 'culchie' used to the comforts and pampering of home. However, the fact that Kerry boys invariably travelled in numbers from house to house made most transfers tolerable and enjoyable, but not always for the other lodgers who classified us as clannish. Safety in numbers certainly existed, but on a more important level when it came to negotiating with the various landladies we were seen to be arguing from a position of strength. As a coeliac with food allergies undiagnosed for years, a 'paiseán' (a delicate weakling) in rural jargon, food suddenly became for me a major issue in all these establishments. Perhaps it was my brothers' experience of the landlady in the South Circular area who reluctantly doled out each individual slice of bread at the crowded meal table that gave rise to initial fears and concerns. For some reason the recent TV advertisement of the Victorian workhouse with its intimidating shout of 'M-O –R –E' occupies more space in my mind than it deserves. Forewarned was forearmed and hard as it was to accept, it took but a few short months for the restricted diet that I had been raised on as a child to be quickly abandoned, as exposure to different foods became a necessity. The choice was a stark one; eat or go hungry. Thankfully fortune smiled as few landladies spurned my offer to assist in the kitchen when it came to washing up the mountain of dishes after meals. Call it an investment if you wish to be uncharitable, but it paid off handsomely on the occasions when the white-headed boy was given open access to the fridge on returning in the early hours of the morning from the late night dances, when the hunger pangs kicked in.

It is important to point out at this stage in the story that all was not doom and gloom on the Dublin student scene as entertainment, diversion and craic were coursed and hunted down with equal determination. This was the period of the show bands; The Miami, Dicky Rock and Brendan Bowyer, and money permitting I graced the south side ballrooms of the Olympic and Crystal without ever venturing to cross the Liffey. The north side meant Croke Park, which I haunted each Sunday after the morning Gaelic matches with the UCD seconds. Goalies were few and far between so I enjoyed a regular game. I learned quickly to stretch the monthly allowance from home with the token 6p entry to Croke Park, a student concession second to none for quality entertainment, combined with the complimentary dance tickets from a Kerry friend heavily immersed in student politics as well as my unfailing facility to gain entry to any event – generally through the back door.

17

Gate crashing, or ducking into theatres and cinemas without paying, all took the sting out of the 'nose to the grindstone' mentality I seemed to have been born with. I counted myself lucky in gaining access to Beckett's memorable Godot production in The Gate and a later Abbey production starring Peter O'Toole, even if the shine was taken off it when a co-conspirator friend was unceremoniously ejected down the long stairs to the amusement of theatregoers. Caught in the act and mortified, he froze and drew attention to himself after mistiming my given cue for entry. Indignities such as this had to be endured and suffered and chalked up to experience. It was an essential part of learning one's trade, as ever-correct timing was of the essence and guaranteed un- detected entry. Morality in such matters never entered the equation, as certain situations required nothing more than a brazen neck. Why pay at the gate when ingenuity could get one in free? This country trait lived on with me for life and as such it was classified as simply living on one's wits, others called it testing the system. Later in life I looked for and encouraged the self same trait in students without apology to anybody. It was a spark that needed fanning, though boundaries had to be obviously respected. Situation ethics best describes this attitude.

During these early student years I enjoyed the freedom of the city on my bicycle, and knew the mountains and the seashore better than any Dub. The eventful diversion of a Beatles riot and The Pillar bombing certainly made life in the city interesting. Regarding the Liverpool group, my interests were limited to the dance hall bands and the music that intermittently crackled through Radio Luxembourg to Kerry via an old Pye radio which never did justice to the emerging Rock scene. I contented myself with Radio Éireann, Joe Lynch and the emerging Clancy Brothers ballad scene. Good Catholic conservative tastes. Only Elvis and his 'Wooden Heart' pierced my limited exposure. None of these could compare however with the short wave band conversations of the lonely and isolated lighthouse keepers off the West Coast who communicated with each other nightly. I eavesdropped on their card games, ring playing, and drinking sessions at September All Ireland time. This constituted my listening entertainment, in a house without a record player or television, which I never saw until I was twenty years of age and studying in Dublin. Life suddenly was attractive and took on a whole new purpose, now that I was doing a steady line with a Dublin girl.

With a teaching post in the offing on graduation, the bird in the hand principle won out easily, and I backtracked home to Kerry with a head full of book theory on how to teach following the Higher Diploma in Education. I liked to think that given time I might prove to be a better scholar in the university of life than in the other academic institutions I had attended to date. I was after all, going from the known back to the known. Had I not sat in those same classrooms a mere four years previously? Even today many consider teaching as a novice in one's old Alma Mater as undesirable, even risky, on the basis that it is better to cut one's teeth elsewhere before daring to venture out on the home turf. On the contrary, I saw only advantages. I knew the strengths and weaknesses of my old school, even with positions reversed now as a poacher cum gamekeeper. Little had changed in the economic climate and catchment areas where emigration still loomed large as one of the many constants of the time. Liberal change was still in the future and in society at large the status quo held sway, with Church and State domination in the areas that mattered most. Big bodies, it was always said, moved slowly if at all. In the skies overhead the Russian Sputnik satellite continued to herald change, as the haunting shadow of the Cuban Crisis receded in a Cold War atmosphere that shunted from one crisis to another.

I knew most of the town pupils, the 'Oppidani', personally as neighbours or through my involvement with Gaelic football locally where I had a certain profile. Neither did I need background information on the country boys, the 'Rusticani', who cycled in from the surrounding areas within a eight-mile radius. A few of the latter group had a foot in both camps as they had lodgings in the town with relatives or friends. The winter rains, poor roads and long morning cycles did not always fit in with a full time education. The annual football challenge in the college between the townies and the country boys eagerly anticipated saw more than pride at stake. One individual, now a priest in Kenya, recently boasted that he was the sole individual who represented both town and country teams coming as he did from the far flung village of Athea in West Limerick, twelve miles distant.

Acknowledging his classical education my classmate, with some element of truth considered himself one of the few 'Athenians' ever to attend the college. Many of these ambassadors from rural areas have been forgotten about, that is until some of their number achieved national status in banking and scholarship, whereupon the town instantly claimed them as their own.

THE LEARNING CURVE

In Listowel, my home town of 3,000 people with a salmon river flowing through it, a large square that radiated streets, education, writing, fishing, football and horse racing dominated people's interests and conversation. In the college I knew the level of expectations, even limitations of all these scholars starting out better than an outside teacher could expect to discover in a whole year. On a personal note I was blessed also in avoiding teaching my younger brother who had left the college in the June prior to my posting in September. Undoubtedly he would have cramped my style and equally I his academic achievement. The presence in my first Leaving Cert class of two specific pupils, four years younger than I was, one a close family friend whose house I visited weekly for a card school, possibly one of the last rambling houses on our long street, and the other a towering giant, friend, and guardian full-back on the local Gaelic team, did not faze me in the slightest. Thus with no small degree of enthusiasm I presented myself on my first day teaching, confident that I knew what to expect, or so I thought. As the weeks passed their presence became a distinct plus, even a blessing, as both in their own individual ways launched and guided me in my teaching. I wish here to acknowledge my indebtedness to both John and Tadhg. Our agreement that the formal 'Sir' applied on the school premises posed no problem. Off duty in the community we resorted to the usual Christian names out of earshot of the junior pupils and senior teachers, as both had to be taken into consideration for different reasons.

Duly equipped with the timetable, chalk and the all-important information on where the cane, bamboo or ' bata mór' for punishment was, I faced into my first challenge, the teaching of both History and Geography to a final Leaving Certificate class. The two-year course I quickly realised had to be covered in a single year, as I could take nothing for granted in regard to the academic information covered to that point. Pensionable and secure jobs in the Civil Service and the popular 'Call to Training' for teaching were understandably high on the priority list of many students in the class of twenty-four, as the cost of 3rd level education was out of the question for most. Year after year many able students were lost to emigration, sadly listed anonymously in the brain drain statistics in today's terminology. Student motivation and expectation never had to be questioned and I was fully aware of my responsibilities. With this in mind I gave them my all, which as a novice, was obviously limited. In truth on their part it was an act of faith and no little charity. It was a classic deep-end immersion, a sink or swim situation for all concerned and were it not for the serious back up and support of other staff members I might not have survived.

The University learned theory of teaching ill prepared me for the reality of my task. If the knowledge and teaching of History proved to be my long suit then Geography was very short on trumps. Any information I possessed was limited to that acquired in my own Leaving Certificate four years earlier which was scant to say the least. Feigning confidence, not to mention competence, in the presence of individuals who knew me was not a serious option. It was here that my student neighbour and mentor, John, now a retired teacher in his own right, came to the rescue as he monitored my class performance and daily progress. He was a discreet and encouraging assessor of my class performance, which he communicated to me in our nightly walks when both our study sessions were over, as out of necessity I was working overtime in preparation for those same classes. It only dawned on me years later the full truth contained in the oft-quoted expression: if you wish to understand a topic fully, teach it first. Never once did John breach the confidentiality of our arrangement, certainly not during the weekly card sessions with his parents participating. Class discipline, which was my sole responsibility to work at and establish, had no part in our understanding. If he was loyal to both sides of this unusual equation it was the measure of the man. This daily feedback on content, presentation and class progress, or the lack of it, was invaluable, without it I would have been stumbling in the dark. He never spared me or held back in his criticism when my best efforts in Geography were found seriously wanting. I can still hear the tension rising in his voice on the school corridor when he tugged my sleeve unseen, advising, "For shit's sake ditch the bloody Mathematical Geography section of the course. You know absolutely nothing about it. Leave it to Mercator and Columbus who knew what they were doing." Duly chastised, this novice teacher followed instructions and concentrated efforts on areas more rewarding in marks. Under this guiding hand, both in and out of the classroom, I quickly learned the art of imparting knowledge, which after all is the very essence of teaching. On many occasions I was reading a few pages ahead of the pupils in the textbook, and struggling at that, a fact that was not lost on the tolerant pupils.

My mentor John, ever present seated as he was in the front row of class, saw to it that the tradition of teaching in the north Kerry area going back to the famous Hedge Schools was going to be maintained, no doubt as it was in his own best interests. The amount of information that John's 'tic-tac' silent language of the racecourse could convey during class with the raised eyebrow, an open palm, a discreet waving finger, never ceased to amaze me. The straight and narrow path was indicated and like the good jockey I followed the riding instructions to the letter. Admonitions became fewer, laconic comments such a 'Doing Fine,' 'Develop more,' 'Skip that,' now sufficed as I grew in confidence. Gradually over the weeks our nightly walks and chat turned more to football and horse racing. I would like to think that after these years he now in turn might claim me as one of those students who benefited greatly from the coaching and advice given. My faltering steps, in his case at least, did not impede academic progress at the end of that first year, which in turn brought him his desired position in the teaching college.

If I was successful in negotiating the initial few hurdles, more pressing and immediate matters threatened like dark billowing clouds on the discipline horizon. Voluntary participation after hours in games was a pleasure to most teachers but the nightly supervision of formal evening study lasting two and a half hours would today be frowned on by Trade Unions. Unpaid as it was, it was considered a tradition and a must for the teachers living in the town, since it was the local pupils who availed themselves and benefited accordingly. As a pupil, I had attended and gained from this enlightened policy by a day school and now, as the rookie teacher, duly inherited the Friday night graveyard shift. In the current climate it would be classified as a Post of Responsibility with payment, and to the eternal credit of all those teachers these study sessions were manned and supervised. Moreover it helped in keeping the academic profile of the college high with a guaranteed minimum student effort, and besides it was an ideal time for the teacher involved to correct the mountain of copies that never seem to diminish. The rural pupils who had returned home, many to farm duties after hours, were denied and certainly missed out on this free-gratis study session.

The nightly scene at one of these study sessions is easy to visualise. With all the class partitions opened a long study hall was revealed where absolute silence prevailed. Visible to all, seated in the centre, the supervising teacher was monarch of all he surveyed. It was in that long corridor, with the ranked students boxed in pews, that I acquired the useless facility to pace the fifty steps east west, head down, book in hand turning instinctively while reading, like a soldier on parade. This scholastic form of square bashing, rarely seen nowadays, not dissimilar to the breviary-reading clergy of my youth who occupied the reserved rocks below the crumbling castle that separated the Men's beach from the Women's on the nearby Ballybunion shoreline. It was there the men of the cloth roosted discreetly in large numbers.

The timetable strictly adhered to in the crowded study hall allotted half-hour sessions for Maths, Greek and Latin in turn, a concession to classical tradition that left all other subjects competing for time. When the teacher absented himself briefly the Senior Prefect was responsible for ensuring that the junior pupils kept the silence rule. It was a strict understanding that any misbehaving individual would have his name reported on a slip of paper awaiting the teacher's return. This invariably resulted in punishment with the cane, a practice approved by parents and the Department. This was the accepted and well-tried system of supervision that prevailed and worked for years. As a rookie supervisor, it was only natural that in time I too would be tested and called upon to honour the rule. It is in the nature of pupils to prod and to probe until they find a weakness. The first few weeks were uneventful and passed off quietly. To a certain degree I had been lulled into a sense of false security but when the challenge came on the third night I had not expected the baptism of fire that resulted. The trap was sprung; the only question that remained now was how would I respond.

Returning to the hall after a brief break I was greeted by the neatly folded paper placed on my table, an execution warrant indicating that the honeymoon period was over. Every head in the hall craned in anticipation. The question had been posed; would the new boy resort to the cane for the first time? I had prepared myself for such a moment, even rehearsed it in my mind. I knew I would follow through with the token slaps of the cane, thereby announcing to the mischievous juniors that I was not a soft touch and would not tolerate messing or any excessive noise reported in my absence. The rule that applied on other nights would equally apply to mine; the status quo would prevail.

However, nothing could have prepared me for the nominated victim; none other than my gentle giant, friend and fullback. The oft-used clichés fail to express the predicament that emerged. A set up; dropped in shit. Sink or swim, checkmate, snookered, even bollixed; goosed if I did and goosed if I didn't. We were both stunned at this hatched plot, which the Prefect and other senior pupils had dreamed up. A foul deed, if ever one was called, that broke all the rules of the Prefect system as seniors were deemed exempt from being reported. With seniority, privileges came. This was high stake poker with friendship on the line. In my wildest dreams I never imagined such a possibility. Fuming, I stood there rooted to the spot, reading the offensive note as all eyes pierced the frozen air. With a deep intake of breath I bellowed out the nominee, insisting he leave the hall immediately. Sheepishly blushing and confused, he exited. I followed quickly, spitting fire. Outside, unseen, I roared for effect so that all within might hear. Embarrassed at the indignity of being put in this dilemma, we continued whispering quietly. We understood and sympathised over our mutual predicament. He took the initiative, explaining the consequences of my not acting. "Call it, I'll hold out, get it over with. It won't change anything between us. Otherwise, you're f…..ed." This attack he said, just as on the football field, has to be repulsed.

What took place minutes later in the full public view of students would have done justice to any Jacobin execution carried out during the French Revolution. Agreed, we re-entered the hall to a silent drum roll, marching to centre stage for all to witness; he proffered his hand in the air. Six times the full swishing cane cracked on flesh, the noise like a rifle shot reverberating from walls and desks where now cowered frightened faces sought refuge. My sideways glance during the second stroke in the direction of the Prefect saw the blood drain from his face. My protector, Tadhg, winced, tears welling in his raging eyes. There was no tokenism involved when the cane cracked six times. I had laid down a marker, a warning for all future occasions. Believe me when I say I was never, ever again tested in that school on the discipline front. My name was made, but at a price, or so I initially feared. The only person to emerge with absolute credit was a loyal full-back whose friendship I had gambled with, but thankfully remained unshaken. The plotters of the prank were shocked and silenced for good. Blood had been drawn, even if I regretted it was not theirs. Composing myself, I resumed my pacing, like a caged lion up and down, stopping briefly once to whisper in a low tone for the Prefect's ears only. I branded him in unprintable words as an outcast, a pariah, and issued fair warning that in time I would have my pound of flesh. His actions as were my words, were unforgivable. I contemplated instead the anticipated joy that unchristian revenge, when it came, would indeed be sweet.

To the horror, even admiration of the students, the hangman and victim, as friends exited the building after the study session in step down the long lit path strictly reserved for teachers. We were making a bold public statement for all the others who witnessed as they slinked down the pupils' path by the wall in the falling darkness. The message was loud and clear; friendship was intact. A situation that could have boomeranged with serious consequences had been successfully defused. Together we headed for the local hotel where the Annual Dinner Dance for the Pioneer Association was being held that night. Tadgh's mother, a local businesswoman, had previously presented me with the two tickets. Suffice to say that the pair of us had a gala night. I bought him a pint later in the up street pub in recognition of his manly and courageous stance, it was only what he deserved. The same sound protection he afforded me on the playing field in crises had extended itself to the classroom.

Is it any wonder then that I requested the presence of this Kerry friend and hero in my 'last hurrah class' after all the years? I was indeed honoured when he graced the occasion as a worthy ambassador of the small number of Kerry students on whom I inflicted myself in my early career.

As for the sinful thoughts of revenge they were harboured and never forgotten, forever waiting on a favourable wind that might see them launched successfully. When the opportunity presented itself I pounced greedily. Twenty years was a long time to wait, but that was all in the future.

A FINAL TEST

If I considered my initiation as a young Kerry teacher now over, I was seriously mistaken. A final test visited itself on me, unannounced, within a short three weeks of the inexcusable public flogging in the study hall. To that point my youthful cockiness and impetuosity knew no bounds. I was now flying free, oblivious of the fact that the white heat of the furnace was about to be blasted again in my direction. Metals on occasions I now accept have to be fired and tempered more than once.

'Cherchez la femme', the French phrase hung accusingly in the air, scarcely audible but impossible to ignore.

Picture me at the blackboard ploughing my way through the history of the foundation of the early Patrician church in Ireland when the latecomer to the afternoon class entered and crossed the floor, scarcely acknowledging my presence. Possibly as a senior pupil, this individual did not deem it important enough for any standard excuse to be provided, certainly not for this teacher a mere three years older than himself. He was mistaken. Quietly and mildly I asked him to retrace his steps, enter again and excuse himself if only in the interest of good manners. Reluctantly he complied. His knock, even if it registered, was inaudible. Conscious that he had a captive audience, he re-entered in John Wayne style, gliding across the floor without as much as a glance in my direction, mumbling as he went some lame excuse under his breath before seating himself. Tokenism with a cynical smile was how I viewed it. By now there was an air of hilarity rather than confrontation in the classroom. Curriculum demands and pressures did not allow for entertainment such as this very often, so the now chuckling classmates enjoyed it to the full. Dissatisfied with his attitude and stance I foolishly requested a final entry, classifying the two previous attempts as dress rehearsals, pointing out the fact that since I had two consecutive classes 'a double' with them, a mountain of material remained to be taught. His third entry was no better than the previous ones I accepted readily, whereupon shrugging himself while standing on his dignity in mid- floor he froze me with an icy stare muttering, "Cherchez la femme." If still waters run deep they reflected the personality of the individual who muttered them. Startled and suitably baited I reacted immediately, surprised initially at my own calm approach and control.

Clarification is necessary at this point. The College, a classical one with Greek and Latin, had no modern languages on the timetable but that did not stop certain pupils from having a passing knowledge of European culture. Many were advanced readers in English and Philosophy and the pupil in question was one; independent, quiet, a deep thinker, struggling with Sartre and Existentialism that I could not even spell, never mind understand. I had picked on the wrong man.

For me the events that followed are freeze-framed forever, in slow motion, as they are also for the scattered classmates who constantly remind me whenever our paths cross. To this day I never know what prompted me to initiate the course of action I took. Neither do I recommend it to any other young teacher. In a snap decision I refused to ignore the perceptive comment, which in my case at the time contained some truth— Look for the woman — I had been indeed looking for that woman in Dublin.

In such small communities it is impossible to keep secrets. My regular rushed visits to Dublin each weekend to visit a girlfriend had not gone unnoticed. Moreover, it was impossible for me to attend the local Sunday night dance halls, crowded 'horse fairs' with over 2000 dancers (our sixties version of the modern raves), without bumping into my senior pupils at the same dances. Hours later in the morning classroom the comments invariably peppered the air, 'A good band last night, Sir,' 'Did you get home OK?' 'Any luck?' all masqueraded themselves as references to the fairer sex and my success or lack of same. Those who had access to their fathers' cars, as I had mine, often ventured twenty-five miles away on such expeditions in support of showbands, only to find me before them. Nothing went unseen. We were indeed cramping each other's styles. I was accustomed to these wry comments, but the French spear launched in class that day under those circumstances, whether the words applied or not, struck home and wounded to the quick.

My cage had certainly been rattled, the speaker was out to undo me, the gauntlet thrown down; I had little option but to confront. When I did it was in the mildest manner possible. Gathering myself and refusing to let my inner rage be seen, I reprimanded him briefly for a minute with no obvious effect. Finally in a moment of inspiration or was it desperation, I stood toe-to-toe saying, "You obviously have a chip on your shoulder. Carry it for life and it will weigh you down. Be like me, a balanced man, with a chip on each shoulder." At this comment the tension broke, he laughed, as did the rest of the class. In the language of the day I gave him the floor, vacating it, promising that not a single word he wished to get off his chest would ever leave the classroom walls.

Confidentiality assured, he took me at my word. I walked from the blackboard and sat in his seat at the back of the class, and awaited developments. The invitation did not have to be repeated. He took the stage. Liken it to a latent volcano, rumbling, shuddering before finally spitting fire. Molten lava poured, gushed and vented itself in a cloud of steam and smoke.

'Who do you think you are? Or the rest of the teachers for that matter! Puffed up dictators, ruling over the masses, riding rough shod on intelligent pupils. Get off your bloody high horse.'

With these cascading words, the introvert had broken his chains and tasted real freedom. For the first time in my life I understood the law of unintended consequences. Stunned, amazed, but above all entertained, we applauded each outburst. This indeed was a virtuoso one-man performance. I bit my tongue. The eloquent tirade lasted not just that class, but beyond and into the last class of the day. The release bell was willingly ignored. Ears reddened; mine initially as Steven's performance attacked and mimicked in turn each and every teacher who taught him in gesture, accent, foibles and clichés. The observations gleaned over his schooling career were astute, accurate and comical. The target characters he picked off like a well-positioned sniper one by one, all were known to me as they had also taught me. A mirror as it were was held up to each absent teacher in turn. The images portrayed, not always complimentary, were instantly recognised. Impressions that we had all formed were conveyed in the strong opinions aired that many were afraid to voice publicly having been denied suitable opportunity. I did not escape his censure though he had limited material to work with, a mere seven weeks. If at times he sailed close to the wind, he always veered off in time. There was to be no shipwreck. I had given him his head; it was indeed a risky action on my part. Was he now playing the clown in this special performance? Had I lost control or gained loyalty? His ability to portray and deliver accurately more than testified to the fact that he was a shrewd observer of humanity in all its shades. He was if nothing else a budding psychologist. Excitement was at a fever pitch on that famous Thursday afternoon. I shuddered to think what the other teachers or sharp-eared student might hear in the next room through the flimsy glass partition, or what construction might have been put on events had confidentiality not been respected.

Looking back, no doubt Steven was lost to the stage. I should have been shrewd enough to encourage him to take up acting in some format, as he was a natural, particularly when the town had a national profile in drama at the time. We were shell-shocked and mesmerised but above all entertained as he waxed eloquent in this impromptu performance, unrehearsed except perhaps in his own brain It was only the repeated opening of the door by the caretaker that finally broke the spell and brought the curtain down on what was the finest class I never gave. I had taken a risk that I could never justify to any authority particularly when the antics and take-off of fellow teachers came close to the bone. Like a river in spate once he started there was no stopping him. If bonding, trust and loyalty were a welcome result, the word mockery also hung in the air accusingly. Never once in the following months had I the slightest problem with that senior group who after that incident worked flat out on the projects assigned to them. I had been accepted and deemed worthy of total co-operation. On the academic front they were gluttons for punishment and deserved their well-earned grades in the state examinations at the end of the year. They had taught me how to teach in a way that the textbooks never could. No matter how unorthodox I was at times they met me half way. True to their word, confidentially was honoured in full. They trusted me, and I them. We had looked into each other's souls and laughed.

It would be remiss of me not to advise other young teachers to avoid similar incidents and confrontations. They are fraught with danger, not to mention grounds for dismissal if school authorities learn of such carry-on. I had played with a fire that could have consumed me and yet luckily emerged unscathed. It took me a long time to admit this fact and yet I again yielded to temptation years later when I should have known better as a teacher of long standing. That too was all in the future.

More than anybody, Steven forged me as a teacher, where in surviving, whether it was justified or not I believed that I could handle anything. Thank you, Steven, and if on occasions I longed for your knock that never came on the classroom door in all the years that followed to convey personally these sentiments, you are remembered with pride. We never again met, and possibly shouldn't.

The two years spent in my Kerry alma mater proved more rewarding and beneficial than I could have envisaged. To the question asked, does it pay to play by ear? I can only reply that in life there are few certainties, only calculated risks.

THE BROTHERS

The two-year stint teaching in Kerry from 1966-1968 can best be described as a finishing school. In that short time the book theory on teaching was tested, prodded and probed and in my opinion found sadly wanting. Had it not been for a willingness to improvise and to take chances, the furnace heat blasted in my direction would have melted me on the spot.

I survived, if somewhat singed, and it was now a wiser and more confident teacher who decided to uproot and head back up the Dublin road in search of another school. I had plenty of reasons for doing so, a girlfriend, further study together with an overwhelming desire to leave the security of the nest and flap my own wings, free from the at-times stifling atmosphere of being known as the local schoolmaster's son. As a teacher, writer, and personality in the hometown he cast a long shadow and I needed space far removed from the bonds, real or imagined, that restricted me in order to develop my own personality. Like any good salesman I did the rounds, hawked my wares and left my calling card in over thirty different Dublin schools, interviewing and being interviewed in turn by the Religious Orders who controlled the secondary system. At the time it was considered unusual for a country teacher to reverse charges as many of the young teachers I knew were more than anxious to return to their country roots, if and when the opportunity presented itself.

Unlike a whole generation of people born in the 1920-60 period the term, 'The Brothers' meant little to me. I was a product of a small town where none of the male teaching Orders ever had a foothold or influence on the local educational front. As a young student I vaguely heard about them, and the closest to meeting one came during the annual visit to the college by the various recruiting sergeants in search of vocations. In truth, in order to be released from class, we often feigned interest, accepted the brochures and holy pictures and excused ourselves from class for a brief chat with the ageing brother who knew well that many of us were dodging the column. If we handed up the relevant material and envelopes at home many a mother prayed and dreamed us onto future religious platforms. It was a much different Ireland back then, as vocations to the religious life were common and no doubt attractive at a time when the educational opportunities for most students were severely limited. Education particularly in country areas was often the only escape route from economic stagnation and free of financial consideration; candidates for the cloth had an inside lane. A comparison of geographical vocation patterns with prevailing economic conditions in areas of the country should reveal interesting data for sociologists. Outside of the classroom on the sports field, the occasional chance comment by an opposing player during an inter school football match hinted that Brother So-and-So would give them hell at half time for wasted scoring chances When my opponents' determination, if not fear, inexplicably seemed greater than mine, I asked no questions.

It was only later when I attended University that I fully appreciated the extent and influence of such teaching Orders throughout the length and breadth of the land. Clerical students, novices and nuns were well represented in the Arts faculties in the '60's, as the front rows of the lecture theatres testified, block booked daily by those with black garbs of various descriptions. It was a different time zone and any young person today will find it hard to accept that when the mid-day clock chimed in the main library of U.C.D., now the Concert Hall, it was not unknown for people to stand for the Angelus prayer. The appropriate cue was always provided by the clerics who thronged the venue, not unlike the Moslem practice of facing Mecca at the appropriate times. If it became a game for those of us with betting tendencies to see who would break first from the traps, it was but a temporary distraction from the books. Initially I followed their example before stopping and shying from the practice in the face of the liberal and economic changes unleashed. Others still were beginning to look east for spiritual guidance. Over time I made friends with many young clerics who played football in College, and my impression of them was that they were content, dedicated and idealistic.

Coming as I did from a family of five sons meant that the influence and happenings in the local convent and girls' school of my youth was certainly not a daily topic of conversation at the table where six males awaited feeding. Nuns, convents, girls' education were a terra incognita to me. Reading about and swotting on the contribution of all these teaching Orders was a very poor substitute for the experience that I then sought first hand in a city school. Any other gaps in knowledge I may have had as a country boy concerning the Brothers to this point, were certainly graphically filled in by my future father-in-law, a product of 'Jambo,' the James' Street Brothers schools in the late twenties. In general he sang their praises and vouched for the discipline, enthusiasm, and dedication of the Order in the early years of the Free State. The subjects he was exposed to and level achieved in first year would put a present sixteen year old to shame. He represented the inner city 'penny-apple-your-dinner's-poured-out' generation who rarely had the luxury of going the full term in school, as most left early to hunt down scarce jobs and become bread winners. The Religious Orders had a noble and proud record of achievement in bringing education to the masses and filling the vacuum left by neglectful and tardy state authorities down the years.

Following numerous visits to Dublin I finally secured a school posting with the De La Salle Brothers in south Dublin, and this filled me with anticipation and excitement in the belief that I was now plugging into a powerhouse of educational thought and best practice. As a young teacher, idealistic, open and anxious to learn I looked forward eagerly to learning from the Order's traditions that had its early roots in Europe. That, together with the close proximity of three other Irish Christian Brothers schools in the greater Stillorgan area, meant that I was in an ideal position to observe and benefit from these powerful forces in Irish education.

Initially I expected a different set of forces and influences to that which I had been exposed to both as a student and teacher in turn in my home college which, though a branch of the county Seminary in Killarney, was effectively administered and run by an all lay staff with a nominee clerical head. It was an interesting fact that the two nearby small secondary schools some miles away in my native Kerry were also lay controlled, a system common to many rural areas where the Brothers had never ventured. In passing, the contribution of such local lay schools in remote country areas has to my knowledge never been fully appreciated or acknowledged, nor has the role of many enlightened educators who set them up in the first place. Professor Brendan Kennelly is one of the few who has indeed paid fulsome tribute to his teacher, motivator and local school headmistress who inspired him.

With an open mind I approached the challenge of teaching in my new suburban setting. Like a football player in the transfer market, I hoped that my club in time would expand and develop my skills and allow me to contribute to whatever success lay ahead. The Brothers' tradition which friends had informed me about, best summed up as idealism, discipline and confident nationalism, held promise that my own education might now be completed. All this whetted a young appetite and confirmed me in my decision that the transfer to Dublin was the correct one. I was happy in my own skin now that at last I had the freedom to plough my own furrow, confident and cocky too that I had gone around the course without falling flat on my face in my initial posting. Buoyed up no end then by a strong Kerry tradition in which the can–do philosophy dominated, challenges and difficulties were seen as opportunities. I faced into a future with new horizons that beckoned and held promise in my new city posting.

And yet on this same horizon dark clouds loomed large. The winds of change that had been ushered in with the Vatican Council in the early 1960's had profound implications for the Catholic Church in Ireland, but especially for the Orders that controlled the secondary schools system, which was then some ninety per cent of all schools outside the V.E.C. sector. The challenge presented by the fast advancing liberal climate, creeping secularism and materialism, even feminism, ushered in a crisis which eventually shook the foundations of the status quo in Ireland, on all fronts, not merely the educational. The new television age in Ireland took the lid off questions that had been scarcely aired, and in the view of many might have been best left that way. A new age was dawning. In the terminology of the time everything was up for grabs, nothing was sacred. Looking back from this vantage point one can fully appreciate the cumulative effect of these changes. Society is often reluctant to embrace change, opting instead to retrench and fight a rear guard action from insecure positions. A brief study of history shows that most change generally follows this pattern. The Ireland of the time was to be no exception. The ever growing media and the TV circus with its new self-appointed gurus, quickly dictated cultural influences on social attitudes and values. One by one the 'sacred cows' that had long grazed undisturbed were chased down; the 1916 anniversary commemorations, the G.A.A., the Church in society, each in turn together with the avalanche of sexual themes became essential ingredients of the staple diet. This was in general a positive development in any maturing society but when institutions and issues were held up for target practice, paraded and discussed in turn by ill informed presenters who had separate agendas of their own, it began to take on the spectre of entertainment for the masses as in the Roman coliseums of old. T.V presenters seemed to wallow in knocking established figures without feeling any obligation to say what would replace them. Tam ratings became an end in themselves. The old was out, the new was in, all assaults could and often were justified under the umbrella of entertainment. Enlightenment and progress in the long run, once the sensationalism died down, resulted from the whole process despite the generation of more heat than light on many an occasion.

This was the backdrop in society for the teaching Orders who faced into a totally unexpected vocations crisis in the 1970's, which resulted not only in a drying up in the stream of new recruits but an exodus of existing members with all the consequences that this shattering development implied. The problem, insignificant at the outset, slowly gathered momentum and before long it decimated religious communities, as vacancies in the senior ranks were no longer filled by juniors, who had veered off the chosen path. A crossroads had been reached. The De La Salles, as one of the smaller Orders with fewer members, felt the full impact of the crisis earlier than most. Numbers dwindled rapidly, amalgamations of schools followed and in time Lay Principalships were introduced to fill the gap in management. This ad hoc reaction to the crisis was probably the only course open in the circumstances.

New plans had to be drawn up for a changed and different world. The haemorrhage of young brothers into the secular world left the Orders shell-shocked and hanging on at times by their fingertips to schools, with the single token brother holding the line. It may be difficult to believe that on a day-to-day basis none of this impacted in my noisy class mansion where chalk and talk continued as it always did, which only highlights the remote position of the isolated teacher. Even when the school grew in number from 100 to 850 over twenty years, the number of brothers on the corridor never exceeded four in number before finally dwindling to zero. As a foot soldier I had my own duties and classes to teach and all the changes at managerial level with the new Boards of Management were outside my concern. In one important respect ever before the tidal wave broke, I was fortunate to acquaint myself with the vibrant last group of young novices, many of my own age who were resident in the main novitiate next to the school and adjacent to U.C.D. which many attended for evening degrees. I socialised with this group of 15-20 young men, attended morning Mass regularly with them in the novitiate, and on occasions registered as Brother McMahon if the Soccer team and Cross Country team in Inter Seminary Leagues needed a substitute to fill up numbers. Living one hundred yards from the school gate as an unmarried man in digs made all this possible, even enjoyable Then again I did not have the pressures and restrictions of community life in the monastery. I was accustomed to hearing the hurried summons from the landlady on Saturday mornings that 'Brother-what's-his name' was at the hall door again. As a group of young men they possessed all the qualities that were admirable; I counted them as friends, and the concept of brotherhood and extended family, attractive in itself, made my transition to city life in those early years very easy and rewarding. How they viewed me was another matter, possibly a needless and unwelcome distraction and intrusion into their religious formation and lives, an upsetting factor and reminder of a way of life that they had abandoned? At this stage I had been invited to teach history privately to the young novices in the monastery, in preparation for examinations for University qualification. For that brief spell I wondered if I was being exposed and influenced by a La Sallian philosophy in a time and climate of dynamic change.

In sharp contrast to other relatively static periods of history, the late 60's and 70's threatened to throw out the baby with the bathwater in its mad rush to distance itself from the relative stagnation of previous decades. Toffler's 'Future Shock' became a reality before our eyes, more prophetic and influential than Orwell's 1984. I can still see the expression on a senior pupil's face as I tried to persuade him to seriously reconsider his priestly vocation, which he admitted to me in strict confidence. I did so against the background and laicisation of three close friends who, in those turbulent years, left the priesthood. My advice given in good faith was only what today's church authorities would counsel. Take time out and decide at a more mature age. Thankfully he did not take my advice, and to date this noted friar and scholar never once held it against me for the advice given in error.

Sadly the educational leadership and influence I craved and with which I hoped to be branded in my new setting never materialised, and with the passage of years I began to question the very existence of an identifiable La Sallian philosophy in education to which I could subscribe. On more than one occasion I visited the Principal's office and asked the Rev. Brother to fly his flag, any flag to which I could march. The firebrand leader I longed and waited for year after year within the management structure never emerged. The brothers I encountered and served under were kind, competent, Christian, but lacked what I describe as fire in the belly, a vision that would inspire others and me. Yes, in my time teaching in the college a steady course was steered that guided our ship forward but rarely if ever was the horizon crossed. We stayed close to shore, hugging the coast, ever prepared to pull into a safe port. I watched and envied on another level the idealism and growing confidence of the Gael Scoil movement in the national and secondary level, wondering whether a similar stream might be initiated in our college. This movement I observed had successfully slip streamed into an idealistic current and when it never happened for us I was envious of the seas they sailed on. And yet due credit has to be given to the managers and our young lay staff in those early years, often acting individually, that solid foundations were laid down in our College that stood the test of time. Future possibilities, beyond what we had as a college achieved, preoccupied me. The six-year cycle of rotating headmasters operated by the order always held out the promise that a Moses would come and lead us. Each in turn, hard working and competent, contributed but there were no burning bushes or mountain fires ignited. So what if I sought perfection and excellence? Didn't Yeats utter similar sentiments? Idealism I eventually accepted could be a curse in itself. If I was destined to be restless and disappointed, even frustrated on occasions, it was a problem of my own making. The secret lay in realising and accepting it – which I never did.

A SEARCH FOR IDEALISM

My failure to identify a philosophy and source the dynamo in an attempt to tap into its energy, led to a deep disappointment. I was unaware if other teachers were of a like mind. Before long I knew that I was destined to continue muddling on without a roadmap or tutor. It was years before a Mission Statement percolated down to the lay staff; in many respects a belated attempt to recover lost ground. At best it was a statement of intent, a pious aspiration, in the face of a new millennium; too little too late. In the maelstrom of change in which they found themselves little blame can be attached to these same individual brothers who in attempting to hold the pass were often entangled in the sticky web of bureaucratic administration. It is no fault of those in charge of schools if so much time, energy and effort is given over to the day-to-day administration. It's a tiresome task, bureaucratic in the extreme that leaves little opportunity to dream dreams. The process has been known to sap the very lifeblood out of the educational system, becoming as it often does an end in itself. It is with some regret that I admit that the idealism and the passion I looked for seem to have diminished. The fire that I expected to warm my hands on had lost its heat. There had to be more to education than this. When teachers in other schools informed me that they had the type of leadership I sought I was filled with envy. As defined by a management executive, leadership has a three-pronged strategy.

1) Idealism, commitment to an ideal or goal.
2) The act of bringing a whole team on board in pursuit of such ideals.
3) The maximisation of each member's talent in pursuit of the declared ideal.

From the start I was possibly naïve in my expectations, and slow to admit the disappointment to myself as long as I had the freedom to initiate what I considered best practice in and out of the classroom. The 'road map' I subsequently introduced and followed but could never explain on paper, was of my own making, best known only to those students who experienced it in my class. I stand or fall on their assessments. With the passage of time certain battles were lost, others won. Was it to be the curse of teaching that the result of the outcome of some battles was never known, at least not in the short term? I was no crusader, but stamina and consistency were possessed in abundance. A nagging conscience constantly queried if this was enough. Realism kicked in on occasions when I accepted that I was a better implementer of policy than initiator. The search for the well of inspiration from which I longed to drink continued. Left to my own devices, self-doubt crept in on realising that what I had introduced was a poor if limited definition of education, if not leadership itself.

The occasional building project within the school down the years rallied support from all and on such occasions a unity was achieved. The raison d'être of the school was naturally prioritised, the education of youth, but at all other times it seemed that each teacher worked privately and isolated behind his own door. When academic targets were reached I still felt that there was something missing. Doubts still lingered. Could we have prepared our pupils better? Were those whom we educated fulfilled in their mission? Were we at times complacent and merely going through the motions? Were we fair and just? Were we critical enough of our own efforts? Did we have sufficient feedback and criticisms? Did we care, or want any? These were the questions that hung in the air week in and week out, mostly without answers. I could don the 'white hat or black hat' so beloved of management teams that swoop on schools, take the temperature and leave platitudes and reports to gather dust on the shelves with the previous ones that failed to be acted upon. Was management mistaken for leadership? In despair I settled for the simple philosophy attributed to the school patron who reputedly did the ordinary things of life in an extraordinary way. If as teachers we joked about this mantra I latched on to it, if only for its simplicity. Like Estragon I continued waiting at the crossroads for a Godot to arrive, inspire, accompany, motivate and direct me along the chosen path.

What infuriated me more than anything else and I failed ever to understand was the acceptance of the 'us versus them', 'lay versus clergy' divide that emerged and persisted to poison the air in the school, and particularly that of the teacher's staff room. Occasionally it reflected the old style management–worker dispute as political stances were taken that clouded discussions and hindered progress. Objectivity was lost, suspicious aroused, battle lines drawn with the ever-present cry of 'No Surrender'. Educational ideas that surfaced from within staffs were often judged not on merit alone, rather on the source from which they emanated. Childish attitudes were struck and worthwhile ideas rejected accordingly, stifling any progress in the process. Leadership in this type of atmosphere was often rejected and where it emerged it often resulted in confrontation. Point scoring ensued and those specialists who revel in insidious infighting filled the vacuum and came into their own. Like infections, apathy and frustration thrived, if not for others certainly for me. Is it any wonder then that the only advice I ever gave to the teachers in my own family was to avoid staff room politics, bickering and bitching? Growth and development under such circumstances is severely limited and well nigh impossible; the students more than anyone suffered in the long run as this cancer like tumour poisoned the school community. Believe me when I say that it lasted longer than it should have. Where small minds dominate it is anything but healthy. From teaching history, which covered Church/State conflicts, one was aware of the end game which in many countries resulted in the secularisation of education. Our staff room discussions were a microcosm of this controversy. Mini victories, farcical at times were chalked up that only a Kavanagh from Monaghan could understand. Insecure authority battled frustrated ambition and jealousy, round after pointless round in trumpeted choreographed bouts. Unavoidably in the midst of these conflicts my mind and despairing spirit were projected out the window on to the rarefied air of Three Rock Mountain, where I longed to feel the wind on my face, careering and freewheeling down hill on the bike at breakneck speed. It certainly was a less dangerous pastime.

It came as no real surprise then that the brothers were unable to hold back the inevitable tide of change with the exodus and decline in vocations. Many of the teaching Orders having fulfilled their main purpose, i.e. the education of youth, facilitated control passing into selected safe lay hands, before reinventing new roles on other neglected fronts, often without due acknowledgement of their dedicated service to Education given over generations. If in turn the various religious Orders sell and divest themselves of buildings and property where economic circumstances dictate what will be the attitude of local communities? Hostility? Will the land speculators gobble again the scarce green spaces? Will the new Boards of Management that currently run most schools play safe and hold the religious fort, or flex secular muscles in the face of the new challenges ahead? Only time will tell. Risk taking I contend can always be justified in any quest for excellence. The imaginative spirit must be free to soar, always conscious that without a vision, a people perish. Hopefully the early dynamism and vision of the pioneering teaching Orders will not disappear altogether in the complex structure of these new Boards.

Nobody can say that the last twenty years has been an easy time for the teaching Orders and the clergy in general. The ugly spectre in society of anticlericalism has raised its head in the context of sexual abuse cases by a minority, resulting in a pillorying of all the men in black. Was it Christian forgiveness that prevented clerical management from acting on abuses when reported, or simply a policy of circling the wagons? The soft option in society of blanket blame for the sins of a few is not peculiar to Ireland alone. Convict the individual but condemn not the tribe. Where blame exists it must be posted at the correct door. Thankfully, in my time teaching I had no contact whatever with any instances of sexual abuse or cover-up. Today the clergy must realise that they have more friends among the laity than perhaps they appreciate. These events that rocked their foundations and ushered in a deep insecurity, partially accounts for the lack of leadership in some schools in recent years. In most schools religion as a topic or class subject in itself has been downgraded and soft-pedalled. Many no longer 'do God,' or if they do, they do so apologetically or half-heartedly. Even the faith schools tread warily in the current climate where religion is concerned. I failed to understand why. When a proposal to build a Cillín or Contemplation Room, a spiritual haven in our school marking the new millennium was put forward and rejected, I interpreted this as proof positive that the religious issue had been downgraded. At best the project was a statement and challenge to counter-balance the selfish noisy bustle of a consumer age. Imaginative drawings when presented were not pursued with sufficient will or vigour in spite of available funds. If nothing else the Cillín would have been a fitting legacy and acknowledgment of the work done by the brothers over the years, if only in the religious field. We owe the generations of brothers and nuns that much as their likes will not be seen again. The spiritual and religious dimension of life that the modern world has turned its back on has to be vouched for. Positive leadership on all fronts, call it idealism if you wish, has never been in greater demand than at the present time.

The new Faith schools that are emerging will be challenged as never before now that the religious Orders no longer have sufficient troops in the front lines. Spiritual values have to be cherished and trumpeted. An interesting development on this subject is a recent statement by the new French President that religion has an important role in filling the moral hole in modern society. Perhaps this attitude also explains why basic philosophy is still on the academic course in French secondary schools. Man does not simply live by bread alone. Religion has to be seen to be progressive and active, not just have a token presence in schools. Certain flags have to be flown high and any reluctance concedes ground to those who attempt to undermine idealism.

If my views were not expressed strongly enough on these issues it highlights a lack of confidence on my part. The Union platform within the College as a structure from which a voice could be heard was a narrow plank in itself, confined as it was to work conditions, teachers rights, even pay. Education committees where ideas could be debated and aired were alas too few in the school and considered precious by some. The few teachers who did Masters Degrees at night deserve credit. But they did so in isolation without backing or benefit to the teaching pool generally. Their class pupils were the main beneficiaries.

In retirement one has time to reflect and accept that this quest for leadership was a futile one. If self-delusion existed hopefully nobody else suffered. So what if I searched fruitlessly for the charismatic individual who would inspire me? In meeting him/her would my boundaries have been expanded? How people would have labelled me would not have mattered in the least, as long as progress was reported. The all too brief influence of a passionate lecturer, Sister Benevenuta, the historian in U.C.D., infected me with enthusiasm, as did the writings of Pearse in St. Endas. These sources afforded glimpses of what I sought. I dreamed the dream of setting up my own school, similar to what existed in my Kerry hinterland, but lacked the courage.

Do the pupils in today's classrooms seek role models such as I did? When the question was posed in class regularly, the answer rarely got beyond the pop or sport star where money always seemed to be the attractive factor. Was I on a fool's errand in a search of this rare species of individual? Was the dream of encountering an inspirational figure a figment of an over active imagination? Do they exist at all? Repeatedly I scour the news items for any references to the existence of educational gurus as the English papers classify them. Was it fortunate, that no such encounter with this much-sought prophet took place?. Had it happened, would I have had to uproot, give up all and follow him? Might he have driven me stone mad altogether as the famous Cork sculptor once put it more succinctly? The question is posed in the half realisation that many of my pupils saw me a good distance down that same road. They certainly had a lot more patience and charity than they were credited with. Then again I had to get old to realise that fact.

SPORT

A hushed silence descended on the lunchtime shop when I entered as the stressed owner attempted in vain to control and satisfy the swarming demands of noisy pupils jostling at the counter for crisps and coke. The pupils, anxious to be rid of me, ushered me to the top of the queue. As a perceived intruder I obliged readily, conscious that this after all was their territory. Suitably impressed, and marvelling at this unusual display of manners the owner queried, "You must teach in the college above, do you?" "Yes," I replied. "What subjects?" "Football, discipline and history, but not necessarily in that order," was the wry if honest answer to the question posed. "If you came in more often it would make my life a lot easier!" he quickly answered. "They are all too bloody fit and active for my liking. What are you training them on?"

Pocketing the purchase and not wishing to elaborate in the presence of a listening audience I exited, chuckling internally on the walk back to school that there was more truth in my hasty retort than intended! Sport, in one form or other, had dominated my life and long been an abiding passion. Had there not been more worthwhile student contact through sport than ever from the blackboard? Through this involvement I certainly got to know individuals on a different level and no doubt they in turn saw me in another light. The strict class disciplinarian was seen as flexible, forgiving, and even friendly at times. The classroom environs understandably imposed strict constraints on relationships, often bracketing pupils unfairly, insisting at all times that growing bodies sat rigidly in confined wooden dug-outs for long hours as their brains were bombarded daily. When vibrating testosterone constantly cried out for the freedom of playing fields and the schoolyard, I realised that it was possible to sell oneself out there as well as in the classroom. Different contacts and tangents could be affected in other arenas; shades of the faded glory of the Eton philosophy.

No, I was not one of the new breeds of Physical Education teachers that launched themselves on Secondary Schools in the late 60's, and yet for a good 30 years I often punched in more hours outside the class-room than the standard class teaching timetable demanded. I readily concede that I loved every extra hour of it and would gladly do so again, with the sole proviso that next time round my efforts would be paced more intelligently.

However had I tailored my energy and curbed my enthusiasm I would not have been true to my real self, as like countless other teachers everywhere I revelled in this spirit of volunteerism, though at times it was an unpopular option with unions and fellow colleagues. Some were uneasy with it, wrongly judging that it was done for self promotion or worse still that it constituted excessive co-operation in the never ending Lay Vs Clergy squabbles that bedevilled staff room politics. The "riches" to be reaped and the friendships forged were incalculable and remained hidden to the small minds that persisted with such views. Was it the lack of internal promotion in the school system in those early days that soured individuals and led to this frustrated ambition in many who had so much to offer? Petty jealousy raised its ugly head on more than one occasion and where it did the only losers were the school and students. It is to the credit of countless "unsung heroes" who volunteered year after year in extra-curricular activities at all levels, as they contributed in no small way to Irish education. Where such spirit exists today it is no longer taken for granted in a money-rich, time-poor culture. Those who participated in games treasure those faded photos on school walls, that is if they hang there as reminders.

Presently it has to be admitted that modern legal considerations might force a person to think twice about volunteering again as innocent circumstances are fraught with dangerous possibilities. Anybody may find himself wide open to a 'grudge' accusation or worse a sexual mis-interpretation as a result of such willingness. Changing rooms on sports corridors, shower areas, even First Aid, all now have to be approached with caution. As a family man it does not bear thinking about. It will indeed be a poorer Irish society if the volunteer spirit that characterised my generation is diminished or frightened off in the face of such negative threats, at the very time when their contributions are needed most by society. Parents, in communities and schools, must step forward, lend their support by involving themselves and not leave it to the dwindling few to preach the voluntary gospel. Sport, and my involvement, always brought a sense of balance that I could not have lived without, as it helped in releasing the compressed academic spring in a legitimate physical outlet. It certainly was not altruism on my part; what was given, came back on the double from pupils at many levels.

In my native county I had been exposed solely to Gaelic Games so it is easy to understand if on my transfer to Dublin that same furrow was ploughed. Had I been brought up with other codes my loyalties might have been different. Benildus as a new school had introduced Gaelic as the main school sport prior to my arrival in the person of a De La Salle Brother, Senan, an accomplished hurler, now a retired Garda on the Border. Glad of my support, we dovetailed our efforts and laid a solid, strong foundation in football and hurling. Soccer was encouraged also at a later stage: how could it not be as the same individuals turned out for Gaelic one day and soccer the next in view of the limited pool of talent available initially?

The rural backgrounds of our small teaching staff and that of the new residents in the growing suburbs of Kilmacud and Dundrum meant that they were equally supportive. Our amalgamation in the early 70's with the nearby Roebuck College, which stood on the site of today's Goatstown Mosque, fused two talented teams into a successful Gaelic squad that quickly registered a Dublin title. The enthusiastic Roebuck teachers and the newly appointed P.E teachers gave further focus and direction to the initial efforts of the Sports Department, proof positive that we had indeed arrived on the football scene quicker than anybody dared dream.

Such were the beginnings of sport in Benildus in the early days. It welded the two separate schools and helped lay down a tradition that still holds strong. On the Kerry scene I had encountered gifted and talented young sportsmen, but to witness on my transfer such an abundance of talent, equal if not superior, was a revelation.

The Trojan work of the local National Schools- our primary feeders, particularly Kilmacud where Micheál De Búrca inspired and drove all before him, made matters very easy for those in the academic and sporting areas. That, and the fast expanding Gaelic club, Crokes, then a junior club inspired and gave focus for the future, once a certain problem that hindered growth had been solved.

If there was joy there was also frustration at the fact that many of our top sportsmen, on leaving the college after five years, were reluctant to play with the local Gaelic club. They had their reasons, which I believed to be related to bad management. Independent teenagers can indeed be difficult to handle. In this context, teachers who spend long hours in their company understand better than most the give and take necessary for co-operation. This seepage of talent, difficult to understand and harder to accept, set at naught the work of hard-working mentors in the college. Consequently I threatened that if matters were not solved locally, I would set up my own club, Gaelic and Soccer, based in the college which would in time cut off the annual supply line of players to a local club with high ambitions. It was a cheeky ultimatum looking back now, but it worked. The GAA club chairman and myself following long discussions thrashed out all the areas of concern to the satisfaction of the past pupils. I was merely a spokesman on their behalf. We came up with workable solutions that solved the crisis, even if it did involve me throwing my lot in with the local Kilmacud club. Since the pupils came from different parishes I had a reluctance to show a single allegiance and affiliate with any specific club, which might later give rise to poaching allegations. My campaign on their behalf was not wasted when over the following period, as a team manager, the refusiniks, a dozen in all, brought the minor Gaelic team to two Dublin finals. In truth these exceptional players needed little motivation or coaching, merely direction. This was progress, but for one of our players, later a Dublin manager, stinging final defeats constituted abject failure. He was justifiably crestfallen.

Many dreams were realised over the years that followed but in truth it was the chase and not the prize that motivated me. A pilgrimage down south to the homeland to challenge top college teams, exposure it was called, proved that our young Dubs could compete with the best.

The infamous high jinks and pillow fights up and down the stairs in a certain hotel in Tralee in the early hours, together with the futile attempts to round up the troops who took a shine to local cailíní after a disco, tested ones patience. Moreover, their noisy nocturnal activities did not facilitate a good night's sleep for the Offaly Senior Team in the same hotel, who lost heavily to Kerry in a vital league fixture the following day. Was this the same team that exacted sweet revenge in 1982? Pass on; it was all part of a learning experience. Realistically it is impossible to prize the self-confidence, satisfaction and sense of achievement that registers on the face of a pupil who realises for the first time that he can contribute, achieve and enjoy at whatever level his talent allows. This is the special gift sport bestows; trust, friendship, loyalty and a sense of well being follow. For all involved in games the dividend is worth waiting for. Out on the pitches mentor and pupil had discarded the masks and stared each other in the eye. A platform and rapport had been established. Words were superfluous. The pupil's latent talent, individuality and independence were given room to emerge and grow.

One can be lulled into a false sense of security and achievement, especially when the dream becomes a nightmare. The politics of games surfaced very quickly within the school and stung more than I care to admit or recall. It was a trauma that left a bad taste in the mouth. Certain decisions and actions thrust upon me haunted me for a lifetime simply because, in explanation to my students at the time, I lied in a barefaced fashion. It was tantamount to a broken contract. Those who really mattered, the students, I walked away from and as a result was guilt ridden for years. There seemed no other option available at the time. How easy it is to justify actions in retrospect. It all seems so trivial now.

For the record, for some unknown and never explained reason, a decision was taken by the Order, in spite of our growing prowess in sport, to replace Gaelic games with rugby. Whether it was done to ape the Southside culture of rugby that prevailed in nearby longer established better known Secondary Schools, or to follow in the steps of a sister La Salle College known within the order as the Sciathán Gallda (The Foreign Wing), I never knew. Naturally any recollection of events is subjective and open to criticism. In this volte-face neither parents nor teachers were consulted in the matter, nor explanations forwarded. Teachers as hired hands in the ranks did not have to be consulted. It smacked of elitism and snobbery at its very worst. Rugby was perceived by some as the game with clout and social status in the jobs market of a Dublin economic backwater. I readily admit to a bias in this regard and reacted accordingly. This bias can be traced to the rugby dances I often attended as a university student in Donnybrook where Gaelic games or 'gaa—ah' and all it stood for, were frowned upon mostly by the ladies, tolerated at best, and explained away as a game for those from the sticks, i.e. culchies. When I invariably walked home alone from those venues emotions ran high.

Yes I was sensitive on the rugby issue, conscious that my allegiance to the Gaelic cause was born out of nationalism and idealism. If it was, there was a lack of self-confidence in defending my position. It was not the game of rugby itself, but the social graces and snobbery that seemed to go with the whole scene that raised my hackles and ran counter to my belief that meritocracy, at least in the job market, was the principle that should prevail in society. To put things in perspective for the reader, the school issue that involved me took place in the time of the Gaelic 'ban' on foreign games, years before the democratisation of rugby that the Munster teams have brought about in recent years, in the time of the Gaelic ' Ban' on foreign games, or the opening of the gates of Croke Park to the oval ball. Neither did it help that the burning debate back then in the media was the proposed visit of the South African apartheid rugby team to Dublin. The passions of many others were similarly aroused in the ever-debated issue of sports and politics. Thankfully in today's world the once entrenched positions of Gaelic and rugby are abandoned, and a welcome accommodation of each other's traditions has taken place.

In the light of all this background when the crucial decision was taken within the school to replace Gaelic with rugby I was seen as a serious obstacle, and put bluntly, had to be side-lined, if not removed. Had the new policy accommodated other codes, even in a minor way, it might have been acceptable but it became obvious that a monopoly situation was going to prevail to the exclusion of other games as prevailed in Colleges with a rugby ethos. Rockwell and Roscrea, which had accommodated hurling as a concession to the Tipperary hinterland, were the exceptions. Regretfully from my point of view, issues were personalised. Open competition would have been welcomed, as all games are beneficial in their own right, but events did not develop along such lines. Regretfully, some of the old attitudes still linger, as a recent tale of woe bears out when a dual player in an inner city college opted for weekend Gaelic in the run-up to rugby cup activities, which resulted in a cold-shouldering.

In the face of the major decision to switch codes, I redoubled my efforts with some degree of success on the playing fields, but the row took a more sinister turn and undermined my approach in and out of the classroom. I came under severe pressure from my employer in the one area least expected, my ability to teach. Innocently I misinterpreted the pressure when it was first applied, but suffice to say that when the heat was turned up I began to question my chosen career. When difficulties were put in my way an S.O.S went out to the people most concerned, Croke Park H.Q., more specifically the Secretary General Seán O'Siócháin. He, more than anyone, was perturbed, as he understood the vital role emerging colleges could play in the development of Gaelic in the expanding territory of South County Dublin where the GAA was poised to make an impact.

The suburban sprawl had just commenced marching from the architect's drawing board. One did not have to be a visionary to anticipate future trends coming down the line. Developers were already smacking their lips in anticipation of land banks. With the exception of junior clubs, there was no Gaelic stronghold in any of the separate districts that looked out on the mountain. I still recall the words by the then Croke Park power-maker, in his early morning weekend visit to the college grounds, on the pretext of walking a dog. Benildus, he stated was central to the unique pioneering investment, the first of its kind by the GAA in Ireland, of £50,000 in a Community Centre now known as Glenalbyn House in Stillorgan, which involved the expanding Kilmacud Crokes club. It was a farsighted experiment in social planning at the time by a sporting organisation. This investment had to be protected – the success or failure of this pilot initiative could influence future policy decisions in other settings. Benildus now became an important factor in their equation; putting it in military terms, the ground had to be held. If I was to be their ear to the ground it presented no problem for me, but any grandiose thoughts of my 'defending the pass' or 'holding the bridge' were ludicrous. In terms of business takeovers I had no board to appeal to or shareholders platform on which to press my case.

In the eyes of others, I was an irritant to be by-passed if the new policy was to be implemented. Yet when summons to the 'office' became more numerous and the screws tightened, difficulties put in my way became intolerable. I finally cracked when so-called anonymous complaints from parents had to be answered regarding my teaching methods. Visibly upset, as a young teacher starting out in life still searching for my feet, I knew the war was lost at a time leading up to my marriage in 1970, with all that entails in housing and decision-making. Perplexed at the turn of events my father, a wise head, interpreted and explained my predicament and the consequences that might follow, and provided me with a plausible exit strategy. In short he stated that in the changed circumstances, obstacles would be side-lined, be they human or otherwise.

In the best tradition of trade unionism, when called to the principal's office again to account for my stewardship, book in hand I demanded chapter and verse on the anonymous complaints, strictly for the record in view of possible victimization proceedings by my Union. The bar was now raised to a new level, in the interests of self- preservation. This action had the desired effect. The specific complaints were finally voiced, chapter and verse; I stood accused of trying too hard for weaker pupils. Incredible as it may now seem, for the first time in months I laughed aloud, stood up and left the office banging the door behind me, but not before saying to my perplexed ashen tormentor, " Carve it on my tombstone with pride." This so-called complaint was and remains the highest compliment received in my teaching career.

In the interests of preserving a career, vulnerable as I was, on advice I immediately withdrew from all sporting activities and surprise, surprise, all further pressure ceased. The unaccustomed long hours after school were spent becoming a DIY expert in my new Stillorgan home, out of harm's way. The whole episode was indeed a salutary experience.

I could never alas come clean in response to the persistent questions by pupils as to why I had suddenly dropped off the sports radar screen. They suspected something but never knew the real story. They could not be involved; they were innocent pawns in a power struggle and turf war. I was after all employed as a teacher, not a sports organiser and so, shrugging my shoulders, and muttering some lame excuses about the pressures of the new life and responsibilities ahead, classes were taught. As a cover story it let me off the hook but it was a blatant lie that grated all down the years. Scalded, wounded and frustrated that my voluntary efforts had not been appreciated I contemplated my future within that college and drafted a resignation letter for the statutory three months notification and re-opened contacts in the Dublin North side on a possible teaching post. Luckily for me nothing came to pass that warranted such drastic action.

The oval ball was introduced and thrown about for a few months but the passes were invariably dropped, as was the experiment. Whether parents in the locality had similar views to mine was unclear. I liked to think I was not fighting a lone battle at the time. It mattered not, as months later before the summer recess, when the transfers and reassignments within the Order became known, to my great joy normal services were again resumed the following September. I asked no questions, neither were explanations forthcoming. I renewed my contract with Sport and continued managing teams for long years after with more enjoyment than success, which is only as it should be.

Round Two of the same controversy took place twenty-five years later following the reintroduction of rugby in the early nineties, on this occasion with a democratic mandate from the teaching staff after a split vote, and heated debate. Democracy was respected, 26 For 25 Against.

At this stage I finally withdrew from managing teams as a gesture of defiance, meaningless in reality but adamant as ever that our existing games structure and traditions should be adhered to. I had nailed my colours to the mast and was too old to change. I queried the motivation behind this change in policy and notified again the vested interests in the matter, stating that another potential takeover bid, or turf war, was a distinct possibility. In time the threat was duly repulsed without my assistance. The College I felt had been targeted by the I.R.F.U., which was their privilege. If I err in my assessment I put it down to an over-active imagination, or possibly paranoia. Confident, wiser and with no less enthusiasm I was happy now that other broader and stronger shoulders on the staff had come forward to share in the workload and pleasure of promoting the existing games of Gaelic, Soccer and Hurling. All involvement in club football locally was curtailed when I appreciated that it was necessary to distance myself from students after the Leaving Certificate. The last thing they needed was their former mentor in discipline organising them on weekends. They had gone from the college, out of my reach, for independence and freedom to grow a distance had to be created. My decision in this matter was not fully understood or appreciated at times locally.

Volunteering as a steward in Croke Park from the early 90's now became the focus of my attention, having re-directed my efforts and weaned myself away from the coaching scene. Sunday after Sunday, first as an ardent supporter with my four reluctant children in tow, then later as an official Maor, like countless others I could be found giving my services in the GAA cause, just in a different capacity. I was confident that those who only stand, wait, and merely direct patrons to their seats also make a contribution, however small, to the magnificent stadium and all it represents, a national focus that any nation might be proud to claim. This was my simple way of giving back to the organisation having benefited myself as a youth from the loyal and unstinting club members, who year after year, organised and trained teams of my generation. Fortunately this same spirit is alive and well today in the college catchment's clubs, Crokes, Olafs and St. John's – and not just in Gaelic. Society owes volunteers at all levels a great debt in the current materialistic age. Would that they could be honoured and appreciated in appropriate ways, as often they are sadly taken for granted. It costs very little to acknowledge and trumpet their work. I admit that I had a limited and narrow outlook on the games I supported, but that is no longer the position. Attitudes have changed, and not least in my case.

****

Certainly sport, Gaelic games and Croke Park as an arena, all at different times pre-occupied my energies and were an important part in my life. While that was true there was one best-forgotten day in Headquarters when I honestly wished that I had been a million miles away after witnessing certain events on Hill 16.

In the context of the Hillsborough and Hysel Stadium disasters even stewards must attend training courses, as all modern stadiums must fulfil insurance and safety regulations. The first historic if infamous crowd scenes witnessed on Hill 16 on the 'Dubs' patch, call it a riot, terrace fighting or whatever, grabbed the national headlines, a major shock to Irish sport, an unheard of event fraught with danger for those supporters positioned there. Stunned, though I was far removed from the fracas high up in the stands on duty I observed all, donned in my identifiable yellow steward's bib of authority. The word Crown Dynamics and crowd control took on a whole new meaning for the stewards who witnessed the scene. CCTV footage was still in its infancy and, if I saw anything with the aid of binoculars, I was not about to make anybody the wiser in volunteering information, which may or not have been accurate, in spite of my stewards' responsibility. Dereliction of duty is what I believe they call it. Privately I justified my action of seeing no evil, filing away the incident while those around me in the stands were shocked and horrified. If questions were posed I convinced myself that a mistaken identity may have occurred. Legal implications may have been involved, so best remain silent. Any doubts that lingered I kept to myself. The incident is a long since closed book, though it stretched the limits of duty and loyalty; the why and the wherefore best consigned to the pages of sporting infamy.

In conclusion, it was only with the rise of the Dubs and the campaigns of Heffo's Army in the late 1970's with all the enthusiasm then unleashed, together with my late conversion to the Dublin cause, that many of my pupils finally understood the full passion that drove me in my early teaching days. Sport was indeed the religion I was reared with from Kerry. The fact that I had 'turned my coat' did not go down too well with my loyal country siblings. This latter day conversion caused me no problems, my loyalty was to my adopted city where I earned my crust! Suburban pupils in those early days had few sporting heroes to identify with outside of cross-channel soccer. I needed no excuse, nor make any apology for branding and exposing them to the games I was reared with. In truth I wanted sportsmen in turn to get as much enjoyment out of sport as I was fortunate to have experienced. Perhaps after all they will now admit that there was some bit of method to my madness in those long gone halcyon days. I rest my case.

JACK

'Can you recall your first history class in Dublin?' the accusing voice questioned down the phone earlier this year. Somewhat embarrassed and dreading what might follow from a former pupil and life-long friend, I confessed to amnesia, and with an intake of breath, I prepared myself. "Fat chance of me ever forgetting, you gave me plenty cause to remember,' he added. 'September 1968. It was the door banging behind me that stopped me in my tracks, first class of the day; you almost took it off its hinges. There I was, performing before class as usual at the blackboard, in this case with a water pistol no less. You stormed in, and with a single look you withered me. Everybody froze. We didn't know what hit us. You simply pointed to the empty seat but not before printing with chalk in big bold letters your name on the blackboard. Like parrots we repeated it three times, louder and louder. By then you certainly had our full attention. 'That's my name' you threatened in a whisper. History is my subject and as long as you are in this school, it's Sir to you. Have we got things straight?' Bolt upright we sat on our perches now fully realising that the messing of the previous year was over."

During the ensuing conversation at Christmas time I warmed to his first impressions and recollections of the once young, energetic teacher. I sighed with relief, thankful for small mercies, that this former witness, now in his fifties had at least sufficient charity to remember me in an acceptable light. Others however had different accounts of the days that followed that did not let me off so lightly. I am nothing if not selective in my recollections.

Jack, line One... calling Jack ... make contact. Please come in. My silent voice within, a cry from the heart, echoes unanswered. You have a different story to tell. It may have been your first day in the college; nevertheless I recall vividly the first time your name was mentioned to me.

Somewhere in that busy world you are still out there, by now a grown man, oblivious that your old teacher wishes to set the record straight. Alas, since you left our paths never crossed, and so the opportunity of settling unfinished business was denied to me. You may still be harbouring demons, even be plagued by memories after all these years; however, they cannot be more painful than the regrets I have to carry. Yours was the first face searched for that night in the crowded room of my last class. I had primed and steeled myself, in the vain hope that you might make an appearance to make amends. It would have been an appropriate and fitting public occasion in the midst of your peers had you allowed me. If humiliation was to be involved it was necessary, for after all it was the very least you deserved. But that did not happen; so with courage renewed, in these few pages I wish to come clean and salve the nagging conscience of old age.

I can still feel the tug on my coat as the father known from Parent/Teacher meetings attracted my attention during the Annual Hurling Competition in the local Glenalbyn sports field. His greeting and brief conversation was totally inappropriate and a distraction, considering the excitement that was mounting in the final minutes of the match in progress. "You have the name of being a strong disciplinarian in that school of yours." Annoyed at the intrusion, thinking wrong time, wrong place, I accepted the half-compliment muttering, "Handy enough," boasting a little in my own idiom, and hoping that would end matters. Minutes later his voice goaded me again, "You will be tested next week by a young fellow who has shattered the nerves of three teachers over the last few years in our local National School. He would break the heart of any stone wall. You will have your work cut out for you, nothing surer." "Time will tell," I replied curtly, not wishing to discuss the matter further. "It will indeed. They say he is going to have you as Year Master and teacher. Three weeks, a month maximum, I give you. He is incorrigible and unmanageable," he added further. He had now caught my attention at the mention of Year Master. I had forgotten that the Five Year Cycle of students had come full turn again and it was my turn to initiate, mould, and expose the incoming 150 First Years in the initial week to my definition of discipline, which hopefully would make the following five-year term in College an easier journey for all.

These were harsh words to describe a twelve year old who supposedly had left a trail of destruction in his wake, and was about to be entrusted into my care. "Don't say I didn't warn you," he muttered. Whether it was a warning, a taunt or a jibe, I took the bait and rose to the challenge. Like a horse whisperer I fancied myself as a disciplinarian; priding myself over years that I had never failed to touch base and bring a pupil around to my way of thinking before again releasing him, like a caged bird, to enjoy and develop his full freedom. Whether it was pride, cockiness, over confidence or the simple inability to turn my back on a challenge that prompted me to say, "Would you like to put a token wager on that three weeks?" With terms agreed and a possibility of our meeting in the same venue for the Football Sevens a month later, I walked away on the pretext of having to meet up with my father elsewhere in the grounds.

Some minutes later I had to retrace my steps to find out the identity of the tearaway and potential terror who was going to make my life difficult. The name branded itself into my brain, or so I thought. It is true that names per se rarely registered with me; faces, gestures accents and incidents forever, much to the great annoyance of former pupils. This lame excuse and half apology was invariably accepted by students, in spite of numerous efforts to sharpen my memory. The latest Buzan technique failed gloriously as did the others before it. In truth, before I left that sporting venue his name had already been forgotten, yet I recall saying to myself that this Jack the Lad was in for a surprise whenever our paths crossed. Thus christened in my own terms he remains, for the purpose of this story, known as Jack.

Refreshed and renewed after the long summer holidays, I always looked forward to returning to the routine of teaching in September. That year was different from others, tempered as it was with the induction by the Year Master in the Hall on the first day back. A new beginning, another five-year cycle, hopefully not the last, to be notched up before retirement, voluntary or enforced; who knew? The conveyor belt, by now streamlined, clicked once more into action. This was autopilot, or so I believed, having so much practice over time.

The excited and nervous chatter of the starry wide-eyed new pupils filled the hall, once the reluctant parents had retreated and waved goodbye to their darling sons. The few traumatised and tear-filled clinging mothers who could not bring themselves to leave chose instead to while away time in the adjacent school car park. In my mind's eye I can still picture myself astride the stage, black gown billowing in the wind from the door left half open for ventilation, puffed up, preparing to fill the heads of the innocent audience with the bluster of a thirty minute lecture before the marshalling of the troops. This Sermon from the Mount was a mixture of dire warnings, clarifications, do's and don'ts culminating in an official welcome and hope that they would enjoy and benefit from their time in the college. This one-man performance from the lofty podium would have done credit to any showman worldwide. I often regret not videoing myself – vanity certainly: what was I after all only a man among boys, temporarily obsessed with a modicum of power.

In due course the customary allocation to the various classes followed on, which simply involved the reading of names aloud. Halfway through the third list, warning bells sounded in my head and the brakes were duly applied. Pausing mid-stream after reading a surname I was jolted back instantly to the forgotten wager made. His former school was cross-referenced on the list; it all checked out, no fear of duplication here. With beady eye I zoned in on an angelic smiling pupil who readily identified himself, immaculately dressed, in every respect a credit to his parents. Inwardly whispering, appearances could be deceiving, 'Was this the lion in sheep's clothing?' His location in the assembly hall was well noted as I reinforced and summed up the salient points of the longwinded sermon, which legions of pupils in the higher classes could have finished had I been taken short. This after all was my one and only long playing record, guaranteed to impact on first hearing however monotonous, repetitive and boring when repeated. Like the missionary zealots in the Ireland of the 1950's I was hell bent on beating the congregation into submission, firing them with enthusiasm before finally raising them up again. Task accomplished, moulded and shaped as clay, the pupils were dismissed into the care of the other teachers who had timed their entry into the hall to perfection for the official walk-about tour of the school's extensive facilities.

Rarely did my eyes stray off Jack once he had identified himself and on exiting the hall I discreetly positioned myself close to him, innocently requesting assistance with some books for my office. Total and eager co-operation was forthcoming as we headed down the corridor with a radiant, beaming Jack in tow, but I was somewhat perplexed that my sixth sense radar screen picked up nothing on our brief walk. Jack certainly should not be underestimated, thinking how easy it was to kill with the camouflage of a smile!

It must be difficult for people outside the educational system to understand how an experienced teacher, as I was then, can perceive a minor in his early teens as a potential threat, even enemy. Trust me when I say many pupils are viewed as such by teachers - not that it says much for the maturity of the senior party in this notional conflict. Umbrage can be taken for the slightest reason, stares and gestures can lead to misunderstandings, all of which are a certain indicator of insecure authority on the part of the teacher. In any overall analysis I know that I passed on the other two great securities of mankind, monogamy and fidelity, being happily married with four children, and on insecure scholarship I was more than aware of what I didn't know.

As we entered the office, on impulse I requested a passing teacher to join us for a few minutes. This was the only sensible call made on the day; coming from a legal family and well schooled in such matters it had crossed my mind that a witness to any proceedings would certainly not go astray. My colleagues' telling of what happened in that office after a few short minutes is certainly more accurate, revealing and reliable than I could ever give, even if he was sworn to secrecy. Banging the door loudly behind me and positioning myself in front of the pupil, I hoisted him bodily by the coat lapels, suspending him in mid -air at the coat hanger level, where I eyeballed him before softly whispering. "Young man, I know all about you, chapter and verse. You have blackguarded teachers for years down in that Primary School. It's over, all over. This carry-on and bad behaviour stops here and now. First and final warning! Do we understand each other?" Desperate situations called for desperate solutions. It spoke volumes for the quality of the jacket worn as only one button popped, as did his eyes frozen wide open in a fixed shocked stare. No dilemma existed about whether he should fear or love me; it was the former emotion I was choosing, in the hope that in time the latter might follow. I believe he spluttered a meek, "Yes, Sir." He may even have been gasping for air; nevertheless it was audible, followed by a repeated nodding of the head, which I took as agreement.

If that was the stick the carrot followed. Slowly I let him down and when grounded again, he was praised for the talents we presumed he had, assuring him that he was starting afresh with a clean slate, and could rely on a fair deal from that moment on. Jack interpreted correctly my finger to sealed lips, a confessional seal I called it. This was our initial introduction and he was assured that any future mistakes on his part would be hopefully rectified with sincere apologies. He owed himself, and his loving parents, that much at least. This latter point I believed to be a clincher because as I ushered him out the door saying, "Good man," he straightened himself and half-confidently stuttered, "Certainly, Sir, I will do my best." Bemused and terrified at this initiation ceremony that First Years had to endure, he thanked me and slunk by the wall up the corridor to rejoin his classmates.

Round 1, I said triumphantly to my dumbstruck colleague rooted to the floor, who later admitted in the safety of the staff room that he didn't know who was more shocked, himself or the terrified student. The whole incident lasted a mere two minutes. An Módh Díreach - direct approach, the old teachers called it, the often effective boot camp approach of the olden days, illegal, brutal and foreign as it always was to Christian principals and family traditions. I am embarrassed to include this printed account as the words stare back accusingly, more haunting than any oral telling. The outcry of 'Sadist, bully, brute,' and 'Guilty' hang justifiably in the air. God forgive me, all I can do now is admit from an aged position that the dictum, 'Shoot first, ask questions later', is indeed an outdated, cruel approach. Are apologies and regrets expressed now far too late? If the tempting whispering voice that rails at today's yob culture still hovers at my shoulder, it does so thankfully ignored. Mea cupla, mea maxima culpa.

Weeks later, in triumphant mood in Glenalbyn, I eagerly sought out payment from the would-be doubting Thomas and critic who had wagered silver. We met, and before I had time to act the Shylock, he half apologetically said that the wager was off. Instantly I protested, to which with a wry smile he said that he had made a mistake, but was still willing to postpone, even increase the bet when and if Jack's younger brother, the real terror, entered the College the following year. The senior brother, he quickly assured me, currently in the college, was a model student; he even used the word 'saint' to describe him being a total opposite to the tearaway sibling who continued to wreck havoc with teachers. Had I come across him yet? The deafening roar of the crowd who applauded the penalty scored on the pitch silenced my gasp and covered a hasty retreat. Now it was my turn to feel the cold sweat of fear. I choked, thinking of the possible consequences and repercussions. Would the Anti-Corporal Punishment brigade, based locally, hear of my action? It was a distinct possibility as they had a daily profile in the National Press at the time. Shell-shocked, I headed for the sanctuary of home; football results were the very least of my worries.

If in life there are situations from which there is no recovery, then this certainly qualified as one. In my case, pride had come before a fall. For months following the incident - a more appropriate label might be assault - more sleepless nights followed than I care to remember. The stupidity and insensitivity of my actions beggared belief. Any good name earned over years as a caring and concerned teacher risked being frittered away, not to mention the psychological damage of the cruelty inflicted on my innocent, inoffensive victim. All sorts of weird scenarios were conjured up as I inwardly defended myself with crafted speeches from the imaginary dock wishing to come clean and make amends, damned if I did, and damned in my own eyes if I didn't.

To his eternal credit, for the next five years while Jack was in my care, the incident was never mentioned or alluded to, he was as good as his word. Others would have milked it for what it was worth, but not our Jack! The sword that hovered over my head never fell. Our secret remained a secret: until now that is, as I am a firm believer that the books must be balanced in this life or the next. For what it was worth, I sought to give Jack every possible break in the system while he was in my care over the following five years .He was showered with sample history textbooks, bus trips, bowling alley tickets, legitimate half days to assist me when I was busily involved organising games, with added special permission to access my office where my extensive library of books was available to him for consultation. How he explained these privileges to the rest of his classmates concerned me not. More than once had he to deny that there was any blood relationship between our families. I believe he fully understood I was trying to apologise without breaking cover. On the academic front he earned every grade on merit, and lived up to the description of a model student before passing on to University where he achieved outstanding grades. There certainly is no doubt as to who learned and benefited most from the whole educational experience over those five long tortuous years.

This then is the reason why now I seek absolution as I still struggle to pacify a conscience that gnaws from within. It's no more than I deserve. As a gesture of respect and atonement to Jack, privately I vowed from that fateful day to have an open-door policy for all students. Transparency and justice would rule, though different reasons may have been forwarded as partial explanation over the following twenty years when asked why I persisted with the policy. The office door remained open until the day I retired, a possible refuge for troubled souls, or so I liked to think. Was I not in turn the very first customer and beneficiary of this lifetime practice?

Years passed before our paths crossed again. Out of sight he may have been, but never forgotten. Appropriately we met in the local Church grounds where he had parked his car in the pre-Christmas shopping frenzy, by now a grown man, distinguished looking and dressed as elegantly as ever. On seeing him I resisted the temptation to turn my bike and cycle off unnoticed in the opposite direction, but filled with the hope and promise of Christmas I approached and addressed him by his proper name, wishing him health and compliments of the season. Taken aback, and laden down by presents, he reciprocated in warm terms. Had he decided to ignore me I would have understood and attached no blame. I was transported back in time when I again heard him utter loud and clear the Pavlovian response, 'Sir.' It was only then that I noticed his companion, his fiancée whom he intro-duced proudly. The warmth of his personality and the extended hand of friendship were more than could have been expected. I shook hands with both, somewhat humbled, congratulating and informing the lucky lady that no other pupil in my long years of teaching had made such an impression on me. This was no tongue-in-cheek; this was a statement of fact, adding he was a model gentleman and a privilege to teach. She smiled graciously basking in his reflected glory. This was the closest I ever came to a formal apology. Had he been alone I was prepared and willing to confess for past wrongs there and then. The opportunity never arose, but his eyes indicated that there was no need, or so I like to think. We parted, and faced into the mad selfish confu-sion that still passes for Christmas. Charité n'a pas d'heure – his charity knew no boundaries. I cycled on and sighed in partial relief as a burden had been lifted from my shoulders.

Recently when I took informal soundings and repeated my story to my lawyer siblings, it is sufficient to say that they were not in the least bit amused. In truth, they were appalled. I cannot rightly recall if mention was made of the Statute of Limitations, but they did say that if charges were ever pressed they would prefer I take my business elsewhere. In my own defence, I stated that I would plead insanity. They readily agreed that on that score there would be no shortage of evidence, adding that they would be only too pleased to supply the necessary proof! Whatever you say, say nothing, an off-stage voice still whispers. Too late, too late as I have now broken silence on my unforgivable error.

Perhaps in this rambling story I should plant clues as to the identity of Jack, if only to head off the stampede of past pupils still bearing grudges. No doubt some have similar type stories; I respectfully ask them to take their place in the long queue to await my sincere and for-mal verbal apology. Time has marched on. What was legal, the norm and accepted in the dark past has changed. The cane, strap or bata are now in the dustbin of history. For many the token few slaps administered for stunts pulled in class scarcely registered in that era. Water off a duck's back. But for the few who suffered torture, mental and physical, the practice was cruel in the extreme and unforgivable. The change in policy and prohibition on the use of the cane never came quick enough for those sensitive souls.

There was only ever one Jack and he was an innocent abroad. My hope is that the real Jack will now come forward and take a bow for extraordinary courage, loyalty and Christian charity in circumstances not of his making.

What of Jack's brother? Sin scéal eile – a story for another day.

P.S. The 'Jack' in question, now working abroad, when contacted for approval to include this story, thankfully if inexplicably, has no recollection of it ever happening, adding that if it did, he is proud to be associated with it!

DAILY DIALOGUES

For those past pupils who meet infrequently and reminisce about schooldays, I now extend an invitation to accompany me imaginatively down the long corridors of a single teaching day.

While incidents and stories transfer easily to paper, sounds and conversations from animated classes, intimate and personal like recordings, echo daily. They have a reality and existence of their own that lingers. These ageless voices, locked within the privacy of my skull, surface and clamour for inclusion. Too long they claim they have been cribbed, confined and caged. They now demand a public hearing. To deny them such would be an injustice. They are a part of me, yet not mine, constant reminders of a Tír na nÓg. Like scriptless actors, unbidden they enter and exit the stage at will, often in jest, even mocking on occasions. In echoing the past, pain and anger register too. As companions of a shared path I have little control over their comings and goings. Cherished and welcomed they dwell within unseen; their splintered notes ripple the air with music. Their song, they claim, deserves to be sung Allow them speak for themselves.

9 a.m. - The monthly assembly.

"Settle down, gentlemen. Must we always hug the seats at the back of the hall whenever we have assembly? I expect more from you 6th years. I know these monthly sessions bore you stiff, but it's all part of the essential housekeeping of any school. Lot's of empty seats up the front here."

"Take one look at our Moses leading us to the Promised Land. Puffed up like a peacock on his lofty perch, himself and his billowing batman gown. It's a wonder he doesn't put on the footlights altogether."

"It has been a long sad month for everybody. We are still in shock; there are no easy answers to this tragedy. We recall Danny now with a quiet prayer. Our Father who art in heaven..................."

"….. Amen. The first of the gang, gone. Nobody should ever die at seventeen. I'm still not over it. He was always a good friend."

"Yes, it's a sensitive time, but life must go on. We must pick up the broken pieces and face the future. The big exam is only months away. It's has been a quick five years since you all trooped into this same hall, chaperoned by parents. Ah well! -"

"Never doubted you for a minute. Exams, first strike. Bull's eye, on cue as ever; now for the monologue. Same old ding-dong."

"The recent survey results on the academic front are interesting, if somewhat frightening. One third of you admit to working well; another third moving up from third gear, but sadly the balance, in their own words, haven't even found the damn keys yet. How or why they ever filled out last month's C.A.O. form, beats me."

"... Blah, blah, you should be surveyed yourself. It's my bloody life, not yours."

"It's never too late to start. You know my views on weekend jobs. Apologies to those of you who are studying and have to listen to this. We know well the price that has to be paid for good grades."

"And boredom is the price paid for listening to you. Don't flatter yourself. The others aren't really listening either. Just going through the motions like you. Get off my case. Get a life man."

" On the sporting front congratulations I believe are due to our Gaelic players, at last the old enemy realise that Southsiders are no soft touch. Hard luck to the Soccer team, in the penalty shoot out. With regards to our dual star player and defender / right corner back, confusing codes is understandable, if unfortunate. No blame is attached if a crossed corner was fielded in the box in the final minutes. In the heat of the moment it could happen to anybody. The culprit will live it down, even laugh it off, given time."

"Culprit! For feck sake, that's Joe my mate you're talking about. Shout it from the rooftops as you're at it, shame him, you're some Job's comforter."

"Adam, Adam. Yes, you down there by the window. You're messing with that mobile for the last five minutes. Texting herself – Again? Sign off pronto. I trust it's not on photo mode. Good, now that I have your undivided attention, I'll proceed."

"Yes, proceed to pontificate after humiliating Adam too! Bully!"

"Now for the ever-important issue of discipline, and the sensitive area of dress code. I'll be brief. "

"Our manners Tsar will now educate the masses. The hobbyhorse will be rid-

den out in all directions. Has he any other bloody jumper besides that red one?"

"To begin: hairstyles. Trust me when I say that I have seen the whole range from number ones, hippie, afro, dyed, mohican, crew-cuts, to today's trendy beards and goatees; all fine in their own time. Now that styles have come full circle again all we ask is that when you present yourself in class, be clean and tidy. As for hoods and baseball hats, all are forbidden, a total ban. If the ludicrous dictates of fashion con and oblige you into wearing sagging jeans, labelled trainers and army coats, civility is pointless. Society by nature is conventional but when conventions grow vicious, aggressive behaviour often follows. Manners make society, not just the man. Poor standards, like an infectious virus, spread and destroy. Without manners we are boorish, destructive and nasty."

"Good God, what book did you get that from? An original thought? That would be a first. Could you repeat, Sir, I lost you at the shagging jeans."

"As for discipline in general, I'll be brief."

" Why stop now? You're on a roll man, go for it."

"Whatever problems we have in our year, we keep in-house. I'm lucky in having a boss who trusts me in this vital area. He gives me a free hand, and you benefit no end. I repeat, we run a tight ship. Problems are defused early; you all know the drill by this stage. If offside you take the punishment on the spot, instant apology or detention. Besides, that way no paper trail is created either which makes matters easy. How long this can continue with the new Welfare Act and the logging of incidents, is another matter. You deserve credit as you have played your part to the full. Hopefully that will continue."

"Too much sugar. He is up to something. Wait for the salt."

"One sour note however exists."

"I knew it. I saw it coming."

"Items lately have been borrowed, lifted, appropriated without permission in certain classes."

"Stolen is the word you're looking for. Spell it out loud and clear."

" Your prefects have brought the problem to my attention. The old solution still stands. As before, we hope the missing items will shortly appear on my office table to be returned to their owners. As you well know the door is never shut, as pupils are in and out of it all day, leav-

ing sports gear and motorbike helmets. Maybe I should charge for stor-
age. The offending pupil will not be noticed replacing the missing
goods. No questions will be asked. Clear your conscience; otherwise
the bush telegraph of the corridor will spit out your name. Then it will
be out of my control. The seventh commandment says, 'Thou shalt not
steal,' not 'Don't be caught.'"

*"He lost his vocation. He is in full flight, fine soft talk. Ask him about the
last fellow who owned up. Bum's rush, out the door never seen again."*

"Enough said on that matter."

"Good."

"Last item on this mornings agenda comes as no surprise and will no
doubt cheer up many. From the last class on Friday corporal punishment ends in all Irish schools. The strap and cane will be a thing of the
past."

*" Hurray! Three cheers! And not before bloody' time! How will you ever sur-
vive?"*

"From the Monday following it will be 'Jaw, jaw instead of war, war.'
For my sins, I made use of the strap and the bamboo in my time, too
much some might say, but it was never personal. As a pupil I was on
the receiving end too."

"That explains a lot!"

"As teachers we are a product of our time, but thankfully time has now
marched on. To celebrate this unique occasion a last public flogging
will take place in the schoolyard, ten minutes before the deadline of
the last class. You are all are invited to attend. Two willing lucky volunteers will be the last victims of a regime that in the opinion of many
has plagued Irish education for decades. You only have to ask your
parents to verify this. Photographs will be taken for the school wall to
record the momentous event. Tickets will be sold, in aid of Vincent de
Paul. This is your chance to make history, by having your name pulled
out of the hat as the last recipient of the cane."

"You never miss a trick, do you? You'd sell tickets in the queue for Hell."

"And to finally balance the books as it were, this Year Master is willing
to be on the receiving end of two strokes from each of these self same
victims. An opportunity however late in the day for certain pupils to
get their own back."

"That's the first feckin' bit of good news I heard from you all the morning.

*Roll up – Roll up. Revenge is sweet, revenge is mine. Make way for the aveng-
ing angel. I'd buy a whole book of tickets for that sweet privilege."*

"Thank you for your co-operation and attention this morning. Remember as students you deserve the very best and where possible the college will see that you get it. I will finish now, as the bell is about to ring.
You will be notified in due course of the next assembly date. Please return quietly to your classes."

*"Good God time flies when you are enjoying yourself. Nice talking to you,
Sir."*

11a.m. - Secretary's Office

*"You got my message. Sorry to get you out of class at short notice. He's ring-
ing back at 11am on the dot. His words, not mine."*

"Is it who I think it is? Don't worry, I was half-expecting it after yesterday."

*"Yes, I recognised his voice. Wouldn't give his name. Wanted the Year Master
only."*

"Was he cross?"

"Very; on the car phone from Cork."

"It happens to us all."

"Want to share it with me?"

"Lost patience in class. Nothing you haven't heard before."

"Don't tell me that you …."

"No. I didn't, those days are gone."

"What so?"

"I balled him out, six weeks waiting for him to get test papers."

"Three months to the exams, that's pushing his luck."

"That was my reaction too. Not an single exercise done by him in the
meantime."

"Well at least you never laid a hand on him."

"Nor really, I just….."

"Just what?"

"I called him up to the blackboard saying, 'Sonny boy, get the bloody
exam papers fast,' and kind-of straightened his tie which was crooked,

at the same time."

"Oh."

"That's when the tears welled."

"And...."

"We stepped out into the corridor, me more embarrassed than he."

"What happened?"

"Nothing. I simply slipped my own set of papers under his coat and said, 'pretend nothing and bring these into class tomorrow, and we will all be fine."

"He took the story home. Obviously."

"Yes, but what version? That what worries me."

"The father said something about him being humiliated in front of the class."

"He would. He has had plenty of practice with the other two sons."

Want advice?"

"I'd appreciate it."

"Storm in a teacup. Not worth telling the boss about."

"What then?"

"Say sorry to the father and tell him it won't happen again."

"You think that's best?"

"I know so."

"That'll calm things down?"

"Nothing surer. I may be secretary, but I've heard confessions before."

"Thanks, you'd defuse bombs on the border; what would we do without you!"

Bhrrr. Bhrrr. Bhrrr. Phone rings.

"He's nothing if not punctual. You get used to them. A real Shylock; I see them coming."

1 p.m. - Oh Brother!

"Brother Pius, Pius. Open up. Are you finished your lunch? It's only me, Tony."

"How well you found me!"

" We all have our bolt holes. They upset you with their gossip, didn't they?"

"I'm used to it by now, or so I thought."

"Take no notice, they aren't worth it."

"Easier said than done. We all teach here; there is no avoiding them."

"They pick on people. It's a game they play."

"Yes, and I'm a soft target. No one told me the rules, me with my hands tied."

"Rules don't exist, they play it by ear. You today, the central heating row last week. What or who is next? They will find or invent some issue to chew over."

"Bloody piranha. Hyenas stalking."

"It was the court case in the paper that set them off this time. No shortage of ammunition there. They never saw you coming in the door behind them."

"A costly cup of tea. Tarring us all, over one bad apple charged with abuse. That got me going."

"You should have given them both barrels. What are they but bully-boys, a breed apart."

"I felt like scalding them with the kettle."

"It's not in your nature, Brother."

"More's the pity!"

"Aye and the other thing didn't help out either, did it?"

"God, but you're sharp."

"You were both very close."

"Joined on the same day and soldiered together for twenty years, we did. He never let on. I'm shell-shocked. It demoralises those of us left."

"Why wouldn't it! No doubt he wished to spare you the pain, as any good friend would."

"Never even took time to say goodbye, it all came out of the blue. Community life isn't all it's cracked up to be. Only three of us left now in the house over."

"Married life isn't either with all its ups and downs."

"That makes it seven in five years, there is more going than coming. Am I to be the last to turn out the lights in the monastery?"

"All told ye did a good job in education even if it has come to this sorry pass."

"I lost track of the last person who said thanks to a brother like myself."

"It was a vocation. You played your part."

"Aye, but the fire's quenched within me. I'm too old to go and half afraid to stay."

"The pupils think the world of you."

"They keep me going. Sure, only for them …ah it doesn't bear thinking about."

"It's depression. It will pass Brother. Give it time."

"I hope so, but not half quick enough. It's lonely at night. I've even stopped praying. God forgive me for saying it."

"Aren't we all the same when the dark clouds roll in? Still, summer is near. You're a born survivor. It will pass."

" And what about the winter?"

"God, look at the clock! I'm down to supervise in the library. You'd want the patience of Job for that mob in there. There's the bell; I'm off. You're OK now?"

"No worse for our talk anyway. Thanks. I'll walk the fields outside for ten minutes. At least the sun is shining. I doubt if I'll bump into that shower, they prefer dark corners, like spiders spinning webs for the likes of me to fall into."

"That's the spirit. Now wouldn't a good blast of Roundup or DDT solve those boyos?"

"Don't get me started again. Be off with you before you're late again for class. God bless. And thanks."

Sure aren't we all trying to function as individuals as best we can?

4 p.m. - Parent Teacher meeting.

"Nice to meet you again, Mrs. Jones; please take a seat. It's Charles, History, that's right. Top of the alphabetical list. No confusion there. Only one Charles, after all. I mean in class."

Nearly put my foot in it there. This will be hard going. A right proper Charlie. House angel, school devil. Whatever you do don't call her Ma'am! Red rag to a bull.

"Yes, his exam results. Reasonable, but falling behind the other pupils of late. Could do a lot better if he really applied himself."

For God's sake don't put the knife in. She is touchy. Doesn't the sunrise from behind Charlie's skull. Dressed to kill she is, all dolled up, don't make eye con-

tact or make a fool of yourself. Play your cards right just like before.

"Will he do Honours? Sure isn't that why he is in Class 5.2? He has the potential but must pay the price with hard work. In the heel of the hunt it's all up to Charles"

Keep it general; use all the old clichés before passing her on to the next teacher. Let someone else spell it out for her for a change. Don't even hint that he is a right boyo. Isn't this her ladyship who attacked the Rev. Brother? Tread softly; stay on the safe path. Don't draw her on you.

"Yes I see. His weekend study is limited by the part-time job. The nights as lounge boy eat into his weekend study time you say. Yes of course it would. Clears € 100 which keeps him in pocket money and clothes? Young people are so independent nowadays; certainly, great credit is due to them. Home, and tucked into bed by 1 a.m., and likes to sleep in till lunchtime Saturday when you take him up his dinner. A mother's love! Of course it's great he has his football matches on Saturday and Sunday afternoons. Taking after his uncle who played for Dublin you say. Why of course you're proud of him!"

Work, sleep, football. I'm half afraid to ask if he even takes the books home at the weekends. Must double check with the other teachers. Minimum effort, token work won't carry him far.

'I agree he is very happy and relaxed about life. No, I didn't know about the steady girlfriend. Met her at the Donnybrook disco last summer and she has her own car? How nice. Of course nobody wants an introverted house swat unable to mix with others. Indeed you are a very lucky mother, why wouldn't you be?'

Ma'am, I don't know whether you're innocent or foolish. If half what I over-hear on the corridor break on Monday mornings is true, God help us all. What would I know; sure I'm from a different generation. And you buy the lads a few cans each to drink in the house after the matches rather than they drinking behind your back? Keep it up Ma'am, it's no easy job raising teenagers, you never said a truer word.

'Yes, Charles did mention something in class about an upcoming foreign holiday. I wasn't quite sure what he was referring to. Turkey, you say. I confused it with Mexico last year. I appreciate it's the slack time in your husband's business and the only opportunity you get for a family holiday. The Bosporus, how lovely. No, I haven't been. Good, you are insisting on Charles bringing his books to make up for lost work. Well done. Certainly I'll try to cover the topics he misses after Christmas again to help him catch up. All part and parcel of a teacher's job. As you say, there is always the Christmas and Easter Grind Courses in the city. Expensive, if it's what you want.'

God give me patience. We have all come a long way from the Shelly Banks and the Silver Strand. Study on his holidays? Studying local talent more likely. Dream on woman.

'What, may I ask, Mrs. Jones, are Charles' ambitions? University? I see. You want him to be an accountant and stay in the family business. Yes, the points are high. It's a tall order, but pardon me if I repeat the question Ma'am; his ambitions, not yours. After all, it's his life to live, his choice to make. Why of course he is your son. I'm certainly not interfering or asking awkward questions for the sake of it, or implying that the points are beyond him. Am I to understand that you haven't even discussed the topic with him yet?'

Now you've done it; you're slipping off the tight rope. Balance gone. Falling, falling, no safety net. She's on her high horse now. Stand your ground you coward, if you dare.

'Most of his friends you say are nice, but there is a wrong element you would rather he stop mixing with. Some of them you say are in the school. They are a bad influence you feel, no ambitions. I see. The crowd up in the—– the place above— the flats ?' Ah to hell's gates with all this beating about the bush Ma'am, the word you can't bring yourself to say is the Council Estate! Now Mrs Jones let's get one or two matters straight.'
— —*Stop. Stop. Too late. Too late.*

'I'm not going to sit here and listen to anymore of this dribble, or have a word said against that 'crowd' as you call them up there. Take it from me, Ma'am, they are salt of the earth, they could teach your Charles a thing or two about manners and life. They are not molly-coddled, and pulling the wool over anybody's eyes. That other mother before you in the queue from 'that place' will have her son in a top class University in England next year. He has already passed the interview. They want him. Cream will rise after all. Pardon me if I say that not all our geese are swans.'

Shit. She pressed the wrong button. There is no going back now.

'I spend six hours a day for the last thirty-five years with young people. I know what I'm talking about. I worry about them. I know everything that happens, sometimes even before it even happens. Trust me, your Charles had better be taken in hand before it's too late. He was lucky with that disco row, could maybe even have got six months for kicking the other student on the ground. They say he spent the night in hospital. You're surprised! I know chapter and verse on the whole story and from good authorities. Money talks. It was all nicely hushed up, if you don't mind my saying so. You're shocked that anybody would speak to you like this? Good! Then you might think over what has been said.'

Oh God, why do I draw down trouble on myself at these Parent Teacher Meetings. Standing up now she is, indignant, shocked as if she has only heard it for the first time. Looking for the boss; I hope she doesn't cause another scene.

'I'm sorry you're taking it like this Mrs. Jones. Someday you might possibly thank me. Moreover there is no point looking for the boss, he gave me up as a lost cause years ago. Your Charles had better be roped in and fast, before it's too late. You have come to the wrong person if it's soft talk you want. I stand over my comments, and that's as gentle as I can be. Pretending is too easy an option; I certainly get no satisfaction in talking like this. The truth indeed hurts at times. It's not as if you don't know already, but thankfully all is not yet lost. If he is reined in and directed over the next six months, who knows he might even get his University course. I'm offering my advice and assistance, because I know he also has good qualities, but I can only go so far unless I get full support and co-operation from the home. Think it over now,

Ma'am. Chat with your husband, and Charles of course. My offer stills stands. Today's date, November 20th, could be a very important date to look back on.'

'Thank you Mrs. Jones for your time; I'm sorry if this is your reaction to my comments. We all want only what is best for Charles. If you don't mind now I'll attend to the next parent; the queue is rather long. Good day now. Think it over. Oh, you are in luck, there goes the Headmaster just passing by the staff room in case you wish to speak to him. Good day to you Mrs. Jones.'

Shit –Shit- Shit. Some people never learn .Why can't I settle for a quiet life instead of starting bush fires and crusading. You're nothing but a voice crying in the wilderness that deserves to be ignored.

7 p.m. – Evening Study

'Good evening, Sir, working late again I see. I found myself passing the school for the first time in years, I'm pricing a big job up in the Industrial Estate so for pure devilment I said I'd drive in the gate and around the parking lot, if for nothing else but to show off and confound those teachers who said I'd do nothing with my life. Mercedes like that out there don't fall off trees. Cars were always my weak point. I'm too embarrassed to tell you the price but I can afford it, the company is flying. Fancy you knowing me after all this time – not that I didn't give you cause with all the trouble I got up to. Water under the bridge. There's little chance of anybody seeing me at this hour though, it's almost dark. I saw the office lights on and I spotted your war-horse of a bicycle, that's what we used call it, parked under the stairs like always. They don't make bikes like that today. I knew you wouldn't be far away. Find the bicycle, find the man; that was our slogan. Sure I had to come in if only for old time sake.

Evening study still going strong I see. Could have done with that in my time. Gives you a chance to correct copies, does it? Nice to see you all the same, it must be going on fifteen years. You're on a ten-minute break according to the lads puffing fags outside in the yard; they said you'd be in the staff room. The prefect will keep order; some things never change. Either hang him or the chatter boxes if there is undue messing, some job for a prefect! You can't beat that kind of remote control. It still works I see. I don't mind admitting, we were too scared to pull any stunts in your class.

You look healthy and fit, slim as ever. Long distance cycling, is that right? Abroad even, well done. I always promised that I'll do that someday, at least the intentions are good. Now that I'm here I'd like to sound you out on something that's bothering me. A bit of advice; nothing new about that says you. You called it as you saw it; straight answers. I admired you for that; it was the lingo I understood. You were the only one I ever told about the whole family saga. You were as good as your word. I still have nightmares thinking about the Court case. When Da died I packed my bags and left. The older sisters went to the States. I haven't seen or spoken to Ma for fifteen years. I have no regrets. She made her bed, now let her lie in it. I know I'm stubborn and hotheaded. The whole episode scarred me for life. I got out to stay sane; otherwise I would have done damage. I've calmed down a bit but not enough to make contact. The old house is long gone; sold, Ma moved out. She is housebound now living on her own in a bungalow in Bray. I have my life; she lives hers. Nancy the sister keeps the odd phone contact. That is her choice. Not a pleasant story is it?

Thing is, my daughter of eight is making her Communion in two weeks time and her teacher said that they can reserve seats in the church for parents and grandparents. Most of her friend's grandparents are coming. The kids are all excited so I bit my tongue and told her straight out that her Granny had come back from foreign parts. The topic never really came up before; at least I avoided it, until now that is.

That's my dilemma for you. So what do I say to the school, or more importantly to my child, Nóra? I don't want her to hold a grudge against me in later years. She is entitled to know her last grandparent. I know what you're thinking. Don't visit the sins of the mother on the son, or in this case the granddaughter. No one wants that to happen but some family feuds never end. At present I'm too busy getting on with my life to start mending fences. Sorry if I'm putting you on the spot. There is nobody else to ask.

I see, very interesting I never doubted but that you would come up with a solution. You think that is the easiest way out of my dilemma? I'd never have thought up that on my own. Let me go over it again to make sure I've got it right.

When the Church ceremony is over, drive out to the house in Bray. Tell the daughter Nóra in all her veils and finery to go up the garden path, knock at the door and introduce herself. She'll have a note in addition explaining who she is, and saying that her father will collect her at the gate in an hour before going up to the Zoo for her big day out. That way there will be no need to meet her face to face, which is something more than I'm able to do right now. An hour should be enough; it will melt the ice at least and get me over my immediate difficulty. It's a first step that's all. Sure I'll send flowers; even get a Mass said for her when she is dead, but I'll be damned if I'll go in person, that would be the height of hypocrisy. The younger generation can speak for themselves, but not for me. One fence at a time; you're right as always. It's good advice, not easily taken, but it will get me off the hook for now. That settles it so, and if anything goes wrong I can always blame you, Sir, just like the old days.

Thanks. It's hard to beat a wise old head. That's intended as a compliment; mind you, we often called you much worse. Ah-ha, hear that noise? Trouble brewing below in the classroom, you must be losing your touch. I had better clear off before I get a clatter too! If I got my fair share back then we only took it from you because you were fair, if tough. I regret not getting to know you better. The only other man in my life, Da, died far too young. Then again, we are from two different generations. Before I go, don't feel insulted if I mention that my best friend has the biggest bicycle shop in Dublin. I could get you a top-of-the-range model for half nothing. Retire that old high nelly - it owes you nothing and moreover some of the new bikes even have batteries for the hills. This friend owes me big time; I staked him in the business when times were tough. You'd look great on an upmarket model. Yes, as you say, it might get stolen. As things stand nobody would dream of lifting that old jalopy. Don't students for miles around recognise it as yours. You'd probably get it back before you even knew it was even stolen! On second thoughts a new bike might give you notions above your station – yes, you have it all worked out, logical as ever. I give up!

Cheerio, I'm off! If I get the local contract you might see a lot more of me over the next twelve months. I'd like that. Either way I'll keep you briefed on how matters pan out over the next few weeks. Thanks again.

'Good evening Sir.'

DISCIPLINE

At the mere mention of the word discipline I can almost hear the chuckle, or is that a gasp, from former pupils now at a safe distance who automatically linked my name and persona with the word. There is some justification for such an attitude, but I would quickly add that the bark was worse than the bite. Myths circulated and senior siblings encouraged them, taking great pleasure in frightening their juniors with exaggerated stories of what lay in store for them, or more precisely, who awaited their arrival on graduation from National School. The standard nickname 'Macker,' associated with all teachers in the city with a Mac in the surname, followed, only to be replaced at different times by Batman – (black gown) and the Cross Country man. All played on the imaginations of impressionable young minds before ever we met. When it sold and created an image in the early days in all honesty it was lived up to though I sought opportunities to allow it crumble visibly when they got to know me better. A wise pupil once observed that it was next to impossible to distinguish bark from bite, as they always seemed to come at the same time.

The word 'Discipline' itself sits easy with me as it has positive associations in my mind and few of the negative connotations that some people, including the young, associate with the word today. With the exception of the one occasion outlined in 'Jack', which is regretted and apologised for retrospectively, I can from this vantage point look myself in the mirror with a clear conscience. I was an old-fashioned disciplinarian; past pupils classified me as strict but fair. This I took as a compliment. When the hard-chaw or one time trouble maker halts his pick-up van or brakes his Mercedes to acknowledge and shout a greeting, or approaches in the most unlikely of venues instead of giving me a bum steer and wide berth, you know that all is forgiven. The word itself can and is interpreted differently, yet without order in the broad, positive sense, the art of teaching I believe is impossible and meaningless.

Over the last generation authority figures have had a bad press, recalling for some the excesses of the hard, cold hand and attitude imposed on others from above. This harsh approach in the Ireland of the past, when the rod ruled at the expense of the heart, fails to acknowledge the countless educators and enlightened parents who successfully struck the right note. Outdated phrases such as 'Spare the rod and spoil the child,' 'I'll learn you,' 'Lay into him, give him the stick,' have to be judged, not necessarily justified, in the context of their time. It is stating the obvious that a certain guiding hand is absolutely necessary for the smooth running of schools and society, and in the absence of same, will even be demanded. The heel clicking Junker tradition with its automatic ' Yes, Sir;' combined with unquestioning acceptance and obedience are extremes that people now naturally recoil from, and still the term was misused to describe these practices.

Secondary schools up to the mid-sixties, many run by Religions Orders, were not immune from a 'One-Size-Fits-All' approach, imposing as it did a conformity that made little allowance for spirited individuals. We have come a long way since then, though there are still a few who harken back to the straitjacket of the olden days, lamenting that with change come losses and uncertainty. Those few instantly recalled in discussions and forever associated with tyranny, were examples of the worst excesses. Irish society and schools have marched forward. Imposed discipline from the top is rarely mentioned nowadays. The welcomed emphasis today is on self-control from within the individual. The mere mention of Rules and Regulations in conversation often makes young people defensive, as they hint at negatives. Even the 'Thou shalt not' Commandments of the Church seem to have been abandoned in favour of the more palatable emphasis on love, charity and respect latent within the individual personality. Does every generation reinterpret and forward its own definition in updating the dictionary?

In our mad rush to be politically correct one has to ask, has the pendulum swung too far in the opposite direction? The now outdated approach of the Church, schools and society that characterised my youth was rarely questioned, never opposed, but always accepted as a fact of life. Nobody today, certainly not teachers, should feel that they have to apologise when they justify the need for discipline in schools. The real issue for discussion is the type of approach that must be adopted in the interests of a well-run school. Individual rights, be they of pupils, parents, or teachers are now clearly defined in law, as is only correct, but where is the corresponding emphasis on duties? Does each right not have a corresponding duty? Is it possible that society may have erred in elevating one at the expense of the other? In today's busy world that prioritises the maximum efficient running of the economic engine, with all the associated greed and selfishness, many teenagers are rudderless and crying out for direction. The constants of the past have collapsed. Role models can no longer be taken for granted.

Over the last twenty-five years a sea change has taken place in society that has impacted on classrooms and forced teachers to assess and re-examine the relationship between teacher and pupil. The fall out in schools, particularly when the ban on corporal punishment was introduced, changed the landscape totally.

The inherited well-defined top-down disciplinary structure now abandoned caught many teachers by surprise, particularly as no coherent alternative was put in its place, at least not in the short term. Many teachers, feeling insecure as a result, were left to their own devices and opted out, choosing to refer problems up the chain of command rather than solve them within the class structure. I never did so and attempted to create in the classroom a safe atmosphere and learning environment within which teacher and pupils might grow.

- The changes in society during this period, which saw authority challenged and weakened; a drink culture, drugs, violence, affluence, and a new emphasis on sex, all visited themselves on schools presenting teachers with serious challenges.
- In the era of affluence and economic growth the traditional status of the teacher in society suffered seriously. The emphasis now was on high salaries; old fashioned, pensionable and secure jobs such as teaching were certainly out of fashion in the eyes of students as a career prospect.
- With the introduction of 'Free Education' the school-going popula-

tion exploded. The emphasis on academic subjects led many to believe that the existing curriculum did not cater for the needs of all. It took time before changes were brought in to accommodate the new demands. Many pupils were no doubt frustrated, echoing as they did the old utilitarian argument that questioned the existence of certain subjects still taught in schools. Were the expectations of many parents, teachers, even pupils too high? In the interests of accommodating all, has the examination system resulted in a dumbing down of grades? Some teachers were overwhelmed by these challenges.

- The false impression voiced in an affluent society that many of the fee-paying schools, boarding etc, had a better education to offer than the non-fee paying sector, was a vote of no confidence in competent and hard-working teachers who witnessed the deserved high grades of their prize pupils registered in the list of honours of other schools they had transferred to for final examinations. Discouraging and ungrateful gestures, for that is how they were seen, sapped enthusiasm. Grind schools emerged; money it was believed could make up for the perceived deficiencies in the all-important quest for university points. There was no bucking the marketplace.

- The family unit structure also came under serious pressure. The millstone of mortgages saw both parents forced into the work market. The 'latch door key' child had freedom and unwanted responsibilities thrust upon him, while many time-starved parents could no longer be relied upon to provide a supportive network for teenagers. In this atmosphere parents looked more and more to schools and teachers who were expected to fill the vacuum left.

In view of all these developments in and out of school, it is easy to understand why many teachers felt that they were on shifting sands. Effective control and order in schools quickly became a burning issue. These background pressures dominated my approach to students at all times, though I was fully aware that there were always more questions than answers. I was forced like others to re-invent my approach and develop an ad-hoc strategy when the cane was abandoned. Time and again I experimented and introduced what I thought would work, hoping that the guiding hand would not be confused with the old type of authority that had been left behind. For the greater part balance was achieved. If chances were taken, in general I was happy when the pluses outweighed the minuses. While parents on the home front tried hard to understand, control and direct challenging teenagers, the struggle went on apace in the classrooms and corridors of school. I was conscious at all times that the challenges faced in a stable economic, middle-income environment were less demanding than those which other teachers were confronted with in areas blighted by unemployment and social problems.

****

It is too simplistic to offer the statement, 'Different strokes for different pupils,' if and when the right note was struck. Some may wish to parse and analyse my approach to discipline, others still question and demand explanation and justification for actions taken. If so, I can offer no assistance. Nevertheless I am confirmed in my belief that if novice and trainee teachers are exposed first hand to the tried and tested methods worked out over years in the classrooms by senior teachers, their task would be made much easier and they would benefit accordingly. This exposure would put flesh on the theory learned in isolation in university.

This now brings me to a topic that has agitated me for far too long. In all truth it is the only educational proposal that I will argue vehemently and defend after a lifetime teaching. Put bluntly, it is my strong belief that the Higher Diploma in Education, the H.Dip., a university requirement for all teachers, is grossly inadequate and ill prepares novices for their chosen career. I base this conclusion on a lifetime's experience and information obtained from numerous young teachers fresh out of college, year after year, who spent their nine months' teaching practise with us. When the initial shock of the real classroom wore off they were invariably critical of the theory they had learned. A degree of criticism is only to be expected but when criticism is repeatedly voiced, it indicates a problem. To be thrown in at the deep end of a Secondary, Convent or Vocational classroom as a trainee teacher with a token three visits over the year by an outside assessor is insufficient.

Too often aspiring teachers are left to their own devices; they are reluctant to surface with discipline problems, opting to struggle on their own rather than request help from within the school, which they believe is in itself an admission of failure. I certainly would have welcomed and benefited from any practical assistance in my initial years rather than be left alone without real guidance other than that afforded by the long-adopted trial and error approach. This method sadly is at the expense of those taught. It demands to be improved by whatever means possible.

Positive experiences are vital in the creation of any teacher. Mindful of this fact I requested regularly that a trainee be assigned to me. There is nothing new in what I was doing as it was a throwback to the Irish Monitor system in the early 1900's. As their mentor I offered them all the practical help, advice and direction possible. Why? I knew only too well that in the early days bad experiences, lack of direction, insecurity, teething problems when encountered and ignored invade like cancer. I know of no survey or study on the reasons why some teachers leave the profession after the first few years. Some no doubt have been broken or disillusioned by the level of indiscipline that exists. Others still remain on in the profession because they lack the confidence to change jobs, and remain disgruntled and imprisoned in class for life. They are a help neither to the students nor themselves in the long run.

Hopefully, in time the Universities or the Department of Education will show real initiative and devise a worthwhile scheme that will train, assess and assist the new entrants. There is no shortage of old hands within existing schools to implement such a policy. The proposal is of particular importance as young teachers are currently assessed for permanency after the initial nine months in their first school. I offered them open invitations to sit in my class on occasions when I would give a demonstration class to illustrate procedures that would instil confidence. This was a sensitive offer for both parties, the recipient in accepting the invitation and the initiator who risked rejection. Open and honest discussion often followed these classes after I in turn sat in on their classes and advised accordingly. Some of the methods and skills were accepted, adapted or discarded as they saw fit. On more than one occasion I was the grateful beneficiary as I copied worthwhile approaches and made them my own. Many were surprised when they were informed that on occasions I had often requested of senior colleagues permission to sit in their senior classes, an open admission on my part that one never stops learning. In forwarding these recommendations it would be wrong to imagine that all new entrants into the teaching profession were in need of them. Many I mentored and monitored were born teachers and required only minimum guidance; other still, a minority, required sustained support and advice, which over time saw confidence and competency increase.

Like them, the only teaching model I ever had were the nine or ten teachers who had taught me over the years. In isolating the good, the boring and bad practices, each was either accepted or rejected accordingly. Few outside the profession would believe that young teachers over a life time of forty years will never again have the opportunity of witnessing another colleague teaching first hand. I do not consider the overheard intrusive voice that booms through flimsy partitions of adjacent classes as witnessing!

One must always remember that teachers perform under the critical eye of sharp pupils who monitor every move, phrase and gesture, many of which infuriate, annoy and bore pupils to distraction. When I regaled them with my wife's story of the record number of thirty-three repeated 'Of course' comments by a teacher in a single class the point was not lost on them. It had taken her classmates three months to prime the pump to that high level before they eventually tired of the class counting game. How much history they learned in that period does not deserve analysis. It came as music to my ears when I learned recently that one of the smaller universities, Maynooth, has initiated a support system for trainee teachers along the lines I have suggested. The feedback to date has been more than promising, and funds permitting, the pilot scheme is to be continued. This is confirmation in itself that I am not the only person with concerns on the necessity to guide and support teachers more effectively in the formative years of their chosen career.

Not everybody can succeed at the first hurdle. A simple structure along these lines I suggest could be put in place for all novice and trainee teachers. The proposal could easily be incorporated into the Post of Responsibility structure in schools. Having been poorly prepared myself by the Diploma in theory and practice, I felt a responsibility to any novice teacher and proffered advice and assistance if asked. Senior teachers with a lifetime's invaluable experience are not tapped into sufficiently and on retirement there is a loss to the system. On economic grounds alone, this is unacceptable. There is nothing precious or secret about the skill and craft of maintaining control and imparting knowledge. However it has to be accepted that the latter almost always depends on good class control.

If as parents we attempted to raise children without worthwhile role models we could be held to account for our irresponsibility, conscious as ever that there is no apprenticeship served in parenting. Education is not something that just happens in schools. The home obviously has a vital role to play but modern parents expect not only academic results, but that the core values of society, selfless commitment, integrity, honesty, loyalty and respect for others be passed on in schools at the same time. This is not an unreasonable expectation though at times it is a tall order for teachers who have never felt more isolated, threatened and undermined in their efforts within the classroom. Many of these concerned parents fail to set boundaries for their own offspring. My colleagues and I took our duties seriously, even if at times the burden was too great. Such unreasonable expectations when visited on younger teachers are unacceptable.

The recent setting up of a pilot National Behaviour Support Scheme by the Department of Education for schools who are willing to identify themselves as having a serious discipline problem is welcomed, as the number of schools experiencing threatening and intimidating behaviour continues to grow. Press reports and teachers conferences have highlighted the increasing problems and any policy that helps younger teachers is a positive step. In any other profession, if an entrant were expected to hone his skills behind closed doors without reference or direct access to a pool of experience, it would be considered laughable.

I do not consider induction by the outside examiner during the current training year sufficient, and sadly I confess that established teachers who, as part of the existing system, hand over two classes a week to these ' Dippers' often withdraw, considering it a free class for themselves, while the new recruit struggles unseen and undirected before occasionally drowning in waters far too deep. Very often it is left to the Principal to carry out a rescue, which does nothing for the confidence of the new teacher. Many promising teachers wind up disillusioned and choose to leave the profession because of initial bad experiences. But this did not happen in the case of a certain Mr. John who knocked on my classroom door on May Day asking me if I could give him some History hours for his Diploma year, starting the following September. At that time of the year all I could think of was the coming freedom of seaside beaches. Half resenting his intrusion, I requested there and then that he teach my class for ten minutes as a trial on any chosen History topic. This did not faze him; he took the floor and launched himself into the Russian Revolution. The initiative shown in hunting down a school at this early stage and appearing on the doorstep was in stark contrast to the piled-high office C.V. applications that arrived in the daily post and spoke volumes for his eagerness and courage. In due course he returned in September – and was I glad he did as there was a treat in store.

******

Pupil: *'You sent for me, Sir?'*
Year Master: 'Yes, Come in and sit down.'
'I'm not in trouble again am I?'
'No. Not this visit, but talking to your Year Master is a good cover story. I've a favour to ask, a confidential matter.'
' You know me Sir. I'm no yard-yapper.'
'It's about your History Dip teacher. He has been with you now for six months.'
'Mr. John, Sir?'
'Yes. He's good, isn't he?'
'The best out, Sir. Nearly better than …..'
'Don't go there …. You learned a lot of history.'
'Haven't we the Irish course nearly finished already, with the Sixth Year still

to come. I could lecture myself on Home Rule and what's more, he made it awful interesting.'

'That's his gift. He came a long way since May last when he asked me for classes.'

'I remember when you introduced us to the "raw recruit", they are your words, Sir.'

'The very ones. You remember too much. His time is up, he's leaving next Wednesday, University exams before the summer.'

'For good?'

'Yes, and I want you to test him. Take him to the brink, throw a wobbly in class. It's his final test'

'You're not serious, Sir – hasn't he passed already with flying colours.'

'It's his going-away present. That, and the special inscribed duster the class can present him with; I have it here. We owe him that, and more.'

'He'll like that. Still I don't know, Sir. It's risky.'

'But I'll be right outside the door at all times, ready to intervene and control matters.'

'It might not go down too well, Sir.'

'It will. Trust me. Use the word 'culchie', object to something he says.'

'If he explodes and attacks me, Sir?'

'Won't I jump in immediately the minute he gets angry? I can see everything through the glass panel.'

'Are you sure, Sir. It's a big ask.'

'I agree. Amn't I his mentor? Who else but you could carry it off?'

'Are you sure he will take it as a compliment when the joke is up?'

'I know my man. It's the highest praise we can pay him.'

'Nothing surer.'

'Friday it is so, double class. After lunch, 2pm on the dot send up the flare.'

'It won't get me into more trouble, Sir?'

'I promise. Haven't I covered your back before?'

'Ok so. Thanks, Sir.'

Friday 2.10p.m. Knock, Knock on the classroom door.

'Seán Byrne is wanted out of class, Sir, by the Year Master on the corridor.'

'For feck sake, I'm standing here for the last ten minutes waiting for the fireworks. What's wrong? Didn't I give you the signal?'

'I got your three separate signals. I did as you said. I tried to throw a spanner in the works. Three efforts I made, but each time he ignored and glossed over my comments. He never took the bait.'

'And I thought you were the man for the job, Seán.'

'So did I! It's impossible to rise him. The class were all gawking at me, wondering what I was trying to get up to. Three times. I fell flat on my face. He's the best ever.'

'I told you so, but I never realised he was that good. Full credit to him; we all learned something.'

' No doubt the best we've had, Sir.'

'That's the end of that caper so. OK, let's go in and make the presentation and fill him in on the stunt that never got off the ground.'

' Please don't ask me to do anything like that again Sir!'

'We both met our match. No point in blaming you. Thanks all the same. We'll go back in so before the bell rings.'

****

'Mr. John, excuse us. Take a bow. I spent a lifetime teaching, and today learnt another lesson. On behalf of the students we wish to thank, congratulate and present you with this token'…..(sustained applause)

THE STAFF ROOM

The Zoo, Bear Pit, The Forum; Junction; Feeding Trough, Clearing House, Pit Stop, Pulpit, Union Chapel and hub – all at various times in the day and year masquerade as the staff room of the school. There too the pungent smells of curry, stale tobacco, alcohol, liniment, damp sports gear, mulled wine, assorted sandwiches, even sweat linger in various corners, all male smells in their own right, constantly competing with the freshly minted books, stencil wax, photostat ink, yielding gracefully in time only to the more civilized and increasingly welcome whiff of perfume worn by the lady teachers.

If one has ears to listen, the echoes of distant voices can still be heard, some sadly departed, to mumble, groan, sing, pontificate, argue, complain, joke, decry, even praise and offer dire prognostications regarding motions, proposals, timetables and official notices. Raised voices and rows over cards, crosswords and private conversations wave-like rise and fall depending on the intensity as salvoes rocket and bounce from the walls to be muffled by cushioned chairs, as the self-appointed gurus and faction fighters, strategically bunkered mid-room, orchestrate and direct campaigns and feuds over half-forgotten grudges that thrive on jealousies, bitterness and bile, insecurities and fear.

The periodic bell on the corridor outside, monotonous and single-toned, unwelcome overall, calls time; punctuates, regulates and directs the constant human traffic of teachers, passing actors, entering and exiting the room, each strutting his/her stuff in the high drama of education at its best, though sadly too at times, falling short. The clarion call marshals, instructs and directs the weary troops, some to the relative safety of nearby classroom trenches, others still banished to war-torn outposts in the loft of the school, a no-man's-land where on Fridays no prisoners are taken.

In this buzzing academic hive workers and drones slaved in service to the education queen in all her power and glory. At times the golden nectar dew-like dropped slowly but when the flow was in spate, productivity boomed, dependent as ever on the mood and temperament of the seasons in the real world outside. In this staff room looking out on the playground, in confessional corners joys and sorrows were celebrated and shared daily. Here again youth and age battled in the ever-constant struggle between health and sickness, success and failure, life and death. Time ticked slowly for some but was stolen from others. On the Wall of Death prying photos, fast fading and pale, stare back as stark reminders of former pedagogues who had in their time contributed before accepting and surrendering their allocated days and hours. Clock in, clock out; enter and exit. In the repeated drama the participants performed for the moment in the ultimate hope that the burden borne over forty years might eventually be laid down on the golden beach of retirement. Yet for some the desired Utopia and trumpet fanfare was shunned in its approach, rarely welcomed and if contemplated at all was done so in secrecy and privacy. Here today, gone tomorrow, missed like a hand withdrawn from water, resigned, consigned, hopefully elevated to a new state of grace spurning temporarily the reaper's sharpened scythe. It was best overall to keep decisions and intentions like the poker hand, close to one's chest. The muffled retreating steps camouflage a silent surrender. Witness too hope in the rising saplings; contrast it with the silent resignation in the felled mature oaks. Internal regrets register, but in the silence of the pruned forest no crash is recorded. In May time youthful furtive glances monitor the bulging post-box nests of the aged colony high in the timber rookery of the staff room wall, where fading forms, circulars and newspapers, elbow for room with the pristine unopened complimentary textbooks of the previous academic year, their spines glistening in the shafting sunbeams splintered by the long-faded yellow of the dusty venetian blinds. Hidden intentions were impossible to read. One lived in hope.

There on the staff room palette the would-be artists in their different hues colonized distinct and separate locations of the overall canvas. The colourful birds of paradise flitted from perch to perch joyful, exuberant and youthful. While in far off remote corners the grey of age fading to white dominated the sombre proceedings, and here speech is in hushed low tones and always private. Age was indeed the passport to this land to which exotic folk need not apply. Lingering nearby the full-blooded red, testified to the active, enthusiastic and sporting clique who persisted much to the annoyance of others at break time, in kicking every ball in the previous day's match; fractionally more animated than the four ball at the other end of the room who missed putts, refused 'gimmys' and plotted weeks in advance future outings and venues. Here and there scattered and isolated, the green mint herbal converts sipped quietly surveying all from their bemused, silent perches, unlike the engrossed crossword and Sudoku devotees who huddled and hunted solutions. Where annoyance existed, it was registered privately. Elsewhere, from their vantage points, the chameleon occupiers dominating the central tables, as ever filtered conversations, darting tongues flicking the air for easy prey. Here nothing was sacred, all was grist to the millstones that grinded and pulverised everything and anything to a nondescript, colourless, dusty, useless powder.

There is no gainsaying this riot of colourful personalities caught in a staff room kaleidoscope. Many flew under various flags of convenience, others ran up the white flag of surrender and settled for a quiet life. All are willing players in the drama of the school staff room, each in turn playing an important role and making a worthwhile contribution, or so people convinced themselves. As in the case of all large families, they lived, and taught in each other's shadow, tolerating and making allowances for each others idiosyncrasies most of the time but not always, as the approaching stressed out voice indicated if one stops to listen.

It was the crash of the staff room door slamming that initially registered the anger and frustration in the incoming speaker's voice as he launched himself, fuming into the almost empty staff room.
"Feck him, feck, feck, serves him bloody well right; had it coming for a long time. That will halt his gallop. The hardest day in the whole week – seven classes in a row, me at my lowest ebb– who does he think he is anyway!"

The silent few within, exhausted observers, took in this Friday tantrum without comment, thinking that the Junior Cert terrors must really have pushed him too far this time. All nodded sympathetically in agreement, not wishing to fan the flames. "There I was, facing into my toughest class of the week. Had he any notion of yielding ground? You are innocent out! Sure he was still going strong, long after the bell he was, with me waiting like a fool outside the door kicking my heels to take over the class. Himself and his bloody History! Nobody else matters. Didn't I nearly have to dig him out with my knocking? Eventually swanned past me as if he was God's anointed."

The interested and amused listeners empathised and waited for the tirade they knew would cascade. "Where do I start? Walked past me he did, as if I wasn't even there, week after week it's the same old ding-dong and when I finally get in and start teaching, what greets me? I'll tell you what! A blackboard covered in scrawl, that's what he left behind for me to clean off. This time he broke my melt! That's a nice example for his students, and he the very man always going on about class litter. A pity he doesn't practice what he preaches! Tells the pupils they deserve the best, but what about me? And he has the gall to call himself a colleague! What did I do? What else could I bloody well do? No way José, yanked his chain big time! Sent out for him there and then, no word of a lie. It took the pupil five minutes to track him down. He came back, he did, all innocent. I stood there, never said a word, and pointed to the blackboard in front of all the pupils who were at this stage agog. Mortified he was. He didn't know what hit him! 'You're good enough to be your own servant,' I said, making a ceremony of handing over the duster. That brought him to heel; bucking he was, fit to be tied. Duly chastened he cleaned it off in a cloud of dust. Speechless he turned and handed me the duster half winking at the pupils, didn't think I spotted it, craw-thumping his breast in mocking fashion as he left. There is no doubt about it but ignorance is hard to beat. I told him to keep the duster for future occasions now that he had learned how to work it. That trumped his card. I bested him sure enough and more the fool I was for not ticking him off years ago. On leaving, he made a meal of thanking me for instructing him in the etiquette of a class hand-over. I don't know whether he has a brass neck or he's too ignorant to be insulted. Anyway, his cards are marked; he won't pull that stunt on me again. The pity is that it took so much out of me; I couldn't bring myself to teach class after all that so I put them revising. I'm still not the better of the episode. How am I supposed to cool down now and enjoy my golf, aren't we teeing off in forty-five minutes?"

As the guilty party beaten into submission, I accepted the reprimand and now armed with a duster coughed, cleared a catarrhal throat and moved on. Possessing an eye for detail and an ear for absurdity, I silently applauded the opportunity seized for creative malice. If guilty, and surely I was, it was within my power to defend myself. But who was going to speak up in that same staff room for the deaf pupil's suffering soul when the grumbling intolerant voices of the few within threatened, when the normal routine of class was upset by the mere presence of a disabled pupil? Accommodation? Forget it. Who dared to defend the disruptive and defiant pupil who through no fault of his own never knew his natural parents, as the wounding label of adoptee was uttered in the privacy of that small world as if to explain all? Rationalism at its worst; nature not nurture. What of the slow trickle of immigrants who in the eyes of some challenged the secure status quo? Limerick of the Thirties alive and well, flying in the face of novenas and 'Totus Tuus' Popes. Cowed courage bore silent witness to the less advantaged, new aspirants to the promised land of milk and honey in the time of the Celtic Tiger. Intolerance and snobbery, insidious cancers when encountered, passed off as Christianity. Noble sentiments in themselves, worthy of all our efforts today and tomorrow, but not just yet. How simple it was as a teacher to knock the dust from a chalky blackboard and wallow in secure complacency. Easier still to gaze on another's wound. Now in the twilight zone memories and faces fade but voices never, some linger accusingly. 'Where were you when I needed you most?' 'Was no one found to plead my cause?' Pass by regardless – not my responsibility. Was that the cock that crew, echoing and re-echoing the past? Did I deny you? Would that these same voices could haul me back to a cherished and treasured youth in the hope of making amends.

Tread softly all you who enter in. Read the unwritten rules. Minority views are the new democracy. You had your turn at the wheel. Cherish the memory of warmer days now past. Cast out cold thoughts. Close the door gently. Withdraw.

TALES UNTOLD

At this late stage of life I berate myself for not revealing and sharing comical incidents, at least with the senior classes. Had I done so, conscious always of the bounds of familiarity that had to be respected, no doubt I would have revealed myself in a more complete way. Was it shyness, political correctness, lack of confidence, or just cowardice that prevented me from doing so at a suitable time and place, curriculum demands permitting? What after all was to be lost or gained and by whom? These questions go unanswered. Scriptwriters for any stage, and I had mine, would classify some of these anecdotes as essential raw material that might be worked up and utilised within a classroom context. Willingness to reveal did not mean that it was wise to do so. At times I saw their potential as possible bait for certain students who permanently stood aloof. At best these asides could be used as building blocks in the bridge-building process, an open invitation to pupils to share in another's private moment. Might they have seen me as one who sympathised and understood their daily struggle? I regret those missed opportunities in ensuring that these doors were kept firmly shut if not double locked in the interests of image. Risks should have been taken, but ego overruled and I opted for the safer path. It is only now that I can laugh at myself, which I wish I had done more of when teaching.

What would my students have made of the youthful "Che" or Shay with whom I had a long friendship? He was certainly a character who made life meaningful and worthwhile. The initial chance meeting with this irrepressible and irresistible young twelve-year-old still attending the local National School was unforgettable and endeared me to him for life. Morning after morning from my groaning saddle en-route to work I monitored the comings and goings of adults and children in the community. It was a glorious distraction from the pressures of school and traffic, besides giving full rein to a vivid imagination. Like the postman or Garda of old on bicycles, I knew my patch intimately. I witnessed change, slow at first, then more rapid as the economic boom and housing market swallowed the open fields and diminishing green spaces. Everything registered on my scanning radar. This impish young Che caught my attention as he reluctantly dragged along the ground a weaker leg and school bag behind him. He possessed a self-confidence and independence that attracted attention. He too was absorbed with his surroundings. I sensed a kindred spirit. 'He made my day,' Americans would say, as I logged him as a regular fixture on the landscape. It was a game I played, matching impressions from chance observations over time, with the real personalities of individuals in the event of our paths ever crossing. There was nothing like prior knowledge, particularly in the case of incoming pupils; if it gave me an edge, all the better. Those I focused on for one reason or another were individual, colourful strands in the fabric of the growing community. Many on whom I had bestowed specific traits and personalities, even invented lives for, like Walter Mitty, escaped and I never met them again. Those of the younger generation I later encountered in school and got to know, often forced me to re-assess first impressions. I stress it was the game not the result that entertained and fascinated me week in week out.

Che was indeed a worthy challenge who demanded attention. The day I passed him busily chalking in large white letters on the gates of the holy Carmelite Nuns, celebrating some soccer victory, I dismounted instantly and accosted him shouting, 'Stop that!' Startled, he did as requested, and then composing himself he approached me in a temper that would do credit to a drill sergeant in any Army. Spitting fire he roared at me in reply, 'Who are you?' Taken aback at his brazen attitude and flaming eyes I huffed, 'I know you, and all belonging to you,' a true statement as I was teaching his older brother. His retort left me speechless and rooted to the road. 'Well, I don't know you, so the best thing you can do is f-f-f-feck off up that road on that crock of a bicycle and mind your own bloody business. Have you nothing better to be doing at this time of the morning?' All this from a primary school 6th class pupil aged 12 whose cold eye stared me into retreat! As passers-by were beginning to gather I withdrew, yielded ground, chuckling as I cycled off chastened. I knew when I was beaten. What else could I do?

Aahh hhaa!! What goes around comes around. Five months later I witnessed the self-same individual visibly shrink and turn pale in the front seat of the school assembly hall during the induction of first year students. Like others, he too had been warned to steer clear of a specific teacher and Year Master. His jaw dropped when he connected the name with the face that now glared down at him from the podium. He needed no reminding. Nodding in his direction, I acknowledged his presence. Interesting times certainly lay ahead for the pair of us. Neither of us was to be disappointed, in spite of the fact that all my first impressions formed were way off the mark. I have no hesitation in confessing that I learned more about humanity from this impressive individual over the next twenty years than I did from many other sources. The tightly knit community in which he lived had looked after an old neighbour and recluse who late into each night scolded her own imagined demons from her shanty hovel behind the roadside wall. As a young teacher walking back at night to my bachelor bed-sit her banshee moaning and shrieking in the yard close to the footpath frightened me. Che in the days that followed filled me in fully on her life story and assured me that the kind neighbours saw to her every need. As her messenger boy and go-between he knew her best. She wanted for nothing except peace of mind.

In time too the Simon Community valued Che's services, as did the landless campesinos that benefited from his coffee-picking expertise in South America. However, it was his final knock on the door followed by yet another twenty-minute lecture on the beleaguered Kurdish minority in Turkey that took my breath away. Current history and international politics suddenly took on a whole new meaning for the mesmerised senior pupils who hung on to his every word. The saga of his Kurdish friend who accompanied him was graphic and gave a ring of authenticity to his account. Discrimination writ large was a more meaningful expression than Belfast up the road. Che's humanitarian and Christian socialist beliefs and approach to problems overwhelmed me as they emphasised justice charity and love, noble virtues that are in short supply in this modern age. He forced me into reassessing many of my own opinions and I was indeed envious of his extensive travels and experiences. He lived in the real world that I merely preached about from the safe confines of a classroom. Any young fostered teenagers in his home today are indeed fortunate to have him as a housefather.

Ever mindful of his verbal assault on me I learned never to judge books by covers. So what if following on this youthful verbal assault I had to swallow some of the medicine I so liberally dished out to students down the years. The youthful Che was indeed a good teacher on that particular day and in time went on to be a worthy ambassador of the college. How much we actually taught him is another question. His regular visits regaled, enlightened, provoked and challenged my own safe assumptions. He will no doubt be glad to hear that in protest and sympathy, mindful of the beleaguered Kurds, I never did visit the ancient ruins of Troy in Turkey in spite of my early classical education. I am forced to settle for Thermopylae and Delphi on the Greek mainland. I still chuckle at the throwaway remark that hung in the air as he left the classroom on his most recent visit, 'Next time India.' Like a gem, it sparkled and tantalised. With the others in the room I had finally become one of his pupils and converts.

* * * * *

If that was a chastening comical story that could have been relayed to pupils a second verbal assault, with expletives too colourful to print and consequences more painful, that followed might have made more interesting telling. Does an expulsion and barring order from a pub qualify as a comical interlude or nightmare? The fact that I was a non-drinker, pioneer, at the time is of little consequence, it simply marked me out as a safe bet in the eyes of others. The reek of smoke that smothered and assaulted the nostrils in such establishments saw to it that I was a rare visitor. The blue ventolin inhaler secreted in an inside pocket for years, an insurance policy, was a constant reminder that drinking dens were strictly offside.

Being commissioned and dragooned at night into chaperoning and riding shotgun by my mother-in-law, a lady, on her spouse and English brother-in-law's visit to the aptly named Magic Carpet for a nightcap, did not initially appear an onerous duty. In my innocence I knew nothing about the eagerly awaited annual drinking contest that took place between Dublin Mickey, and London Jimmy. Picture me, ill prepared as I was, pig in the middle, staunch member of the soft drinks brigade now elevated to the status of scorekeeper and referee, between willing participants running free from the clutches of their women-folk. Round after round, all very civilised, this bored onlooker tallied and logged the score on conveniently placed bar coasters. The long established ground rules, I was informed, were again in operation, with the oft-repeated mantra 'Two pints equals a double whiskey,' testing my counting skills. In the 'Fanta' time it took me to sip and sup three bottles, they eyeballed each other over the tilting rims of emptied glasses. Nobody blinked; garrulous and good-humoured the banter echoed. They scarcely acknowledged my presence. When a nature call, timeout, was requested by London Jim, the gesture was taken as a partial retreat by the Liberties representative, weaned since birth on brewery air, still warming to the task. As London's finest launched himself on the long voyage to the rest room it was obvious that he had not found his sea legs, as the ballast tanks listed noticeably and radar malfunctioned. Sharpen your pencil, I was instructed by my in-law, because in the second half the serious drinking would begin.

The inexplicable five-minute absence from the table resulted in a referee's visit to the dressing room to investigate the delay in proceedings. If the signs were ominous nothing could have prepared me for the scene that followed. Prostrate on the floor, half in, half out of the urinal, mumbling incoherently, glasses broken, blood oozing, the old enemy had succumbed. Seeing me he began to serenade with an old English ditty. As a Good Samaritan I offered assistance, bending down to lift him up just in time to see the shocked face of the next would-be visitor to the boys' room freeze-framed in the half-opened doorway. A momentary glance in my direction, a jumped conclusion, resulted in a fast retreat to loud shouts of 'Mugging. Mugging, Help'. Rooted to the spot I was speechless, suddenly hoisted bodily, limbs dangling in midair by two burly barmen and frogmarched through the jeering crowd only to be pitched unceremoniously on the pavement outside with a good old-fashioned rooter up the arse. I distinctly recall hearing in my agitated state 'Barred for life; shag off you bastard and low type. Never again darken our door, try that on for size,' as another kick missed the painful spot by inches.

Circumstances had again conspired against me but I lived it down, only slightly embarrassed. If I laughed heartily the following day I certainly lost no sleep over it; after all it was a memorable highlight of an Englishman's visit, which I was never allowed to forget. While it did not drive me to drink, Seven Up became my preferred choice. The colourful and ringing expletives hurled at me on those two occasions had the desired effect, as from that time out I vowed never again to challenge youthful individuals or darken the door of pubs.

When tales and anecdotes like these went untold in class, it was due to a shyness on my part. Were these missed opportunities to forge closer relationships? They certainly gave a whole new understanding to first impressions, jumped conclusions, expulsions, rash judgements – even punishments – all common currency of a school day.

THE TEN PER CENT

I readily accept that the current structure and disciplinary procedures operating in most schools more than adequately cater for the ninety percent of students on a daily basis. This group progress normally through the educational system, develop their potential, assert their individuality and even enjoy themselves before going out to live their lives confidently in society. The regular student has at most to be taught and directed by competent teachers. However, the remaining ten per cent must be catered for if not prioritised in what I term a Bridge Building exercise if they are to benefit. Some fail for a variety of reasons to integrate and develop, are unmotivated and often out of kilter with their surroundings, especially when labelled as troublemakers when ground rules are not adhered to.

As a rule the course content of the subject taught is a sufficient contact between pupil and teacher across which a trusting relationship can be established. However, this did not carry over in my experience to the precious minority group, whose academic ability might range across the spectrum. The general approach was insufficient and it was necessary to reach out and go the extra mile for these off-side pupils before trust, confidence and rapport were established. The barricades they build and man successfully often repulse the probing advances of concerned and helpful teachers. The casual cold eye and dismissive shoulder shrug invariably saw off many a willing Samaritan. In time they were processed by the system, tolerated without benefiting to the full. Any individual fall-out, dropout, loss or expulsion was for me disturbing and sad, if not an overall admission of failure on all our parts. Was this after all the survival of the fittest dictum, in operation?

When my concerns went unresolved I agonised in vain. Silently fuming I blamed myself for the inadequate help given, watching their lonely outposts from afar. Secretly tracking their progress in later years, silent cheers registered if they prospered in business, hurt alas too often when the individual flame flickered and was extinguished in the crazy, impatient, uncaring climate of the then emerging Celtic Tiger.

Half-heartedly the sentiments of others were echoed that we were there to teach and not solve the problems that modern society visited on our school. As a reaction to this situation, courage was found to zone in quietly and unnoticed in a bridge-building approach, aware that there was nothing unique in what I was doing. This exercise needs no explanation for any teacher involved in any after-hours activities who appreciates the fact that non-class contact offers ideal opportunities.

The reasons why they under-achieved, lacked self-esteem and self-confidence were complex, but with a bridge established they slowly appreciated that they were not written off and that others cared about them. In an age of mass communication and technology the inability of many students to verbalise or communicate is a major obstacle, as is the unwillingness and deafness of adults and society to hear their silent screams. Alas it was always too late for those few when they sadly registered as statistics in the death columns of the newspaper. Nothing haunted me more in teaching than this possibility, as guilt hovered close as an unwelcome visitor.

As teachers, from time to time in different ways we fail pupils on the academic treadmill. Repeated efforts were made to establish contact when and if it looked necessary to do so. Success or no, it indicated concern, which was sufficient for certain individuals. It was a comforting thought also to know that other teachers were reacting to similar distress signals over-looked by me. As a class teacher, games mentor and Year Head there certainly was no shortage of bridge-building opportunities.

10 a.m - School corridor.

"So you came in after all?"
"Yes, Sir. I was too embarrassed to come in till you sent out word to meet you on the bridge."
"Tom was slow to part with your mobile number."
"That's what a friend is supposed to do."

"For a while there I thought I was wasting my time. Didn't think you were turning up. It was cold up there."

 "No one saw us, Sir, the trees at the bridge provide cover. I thought over what you said."

"Good, you are giving it another go so. We all make mistakes."

 "I'll try, Sir. I've had my fill of stomach pumps."

" Good man. Down you go now. Sneak in by the sports door at small break. If anybody says anything, say you had an office appointment with me."

 "Is that what they call a white lie, Sir?"

"Now, now. Enough said. Keep your nose clean and lie low for a while."

 "Thanks, Sir."

Two hours later. 12a.m. Outside classroom door.

"For feck sake, not again! Who threw you out this time?"

 "Mr. Moloney Sir. I was only just ...."

"Shut up! If I hear that 'just only' excuse once more I'll have a fit. Just only messing in class. How many others did he warn?"

 "Two, Sir."

"And you were the third?"

 "Sorry, Sir."

"Serves you bloody well right. You never learn. What age are you now?"

 "Seventeen and a half, Sir."

"Leaving school in five months. Is this the best you can do? What day is it today?"

 "Friday – afternoon."

"And if the boss catches you here, what happens?"

 "Detention. Saturday, Sir."

"Cut out the Sir business … And?"

 .*"Grounded again by my parents. Ma and Da will give up on me."*

"And?"

 "And loose my place on the school team."

"What do I say about Fridays?"

 "Everybody is shagged by the end of the week. Patience is scarce. Lie low."

"At least we taught you that much."

"I'm sorry, Sir."

"Sir my arse! It's respect we are talking about here. Now you have me cursing. You're saying sorry to the wrong bloody man."

"I know, Sir."

"Listen to me, can you keep a secret? Man to man. A real secret? No blabbering? Just the two of us?"

"Of course, Sir."

"Mr. Maloney's wife is very sick in hospital."

"Didn't know, Sir."

"You're not supposed to bloody well know! Remember that! And last year, what about your Da's heart attack, we made allowances when you threw the head didn't we?"

"I know Sir. I appreciate it."

"Does that change matters now?"

"It should, Sir."

"Good. You know the solution so?"

"Knock. Apologise and mean it."

"That is if he'll accept the apology. Otherwise you're in hot water up to your sweet neck."

"I understand Sir."

'Trust me now. In you go and make a good job of it; that might put us all in the clear."

"I'll try my best."

"Take a good deep breath. It will be all over in sixty seconds. I'll nip around the corner here out of sight just to make sure nothing goes wrong. But first, I have to bawl you out for the crowd inside to hear. Strictly sound effects. Then I'll have to shake you, bang the door even, pure act. Can you play along?"

"No problem, Sir."

Roars. Bang. Knock. Entry. Muffled voices. Exit again.

"For shit's sake what went wrong now, you're out again!"

"Didn't I forget my school bag? It worked. I'm off the hook. By the way Sir, it only took thirty-eight seconds. Thanks."

The life long commitment I made to bridging was more rewarding, when successful, than any classroom effort. It entailed close observation of individuals from a distance at first, the registering of mood swings, reading faces, picking up signals and vibes, monitoring of interaction if any with friends, and finally the unearthing of talents, interests, even obsessions. All this accumulated information helped to give a bigger picture to the silent, aloof pose struck in class. Implicit in all of this is the fact that the individuality of each person had to be respected. There could be no barging in on any private world.

Once tentative contact was made, entry was strictly at the invitation of the student; it was up to him to take up or reject the overtures and assistance offered. If trust was established, mutual respect soon followed which often led to open communication on problems, ambitions, even secrets. With this essential breakthrough, the oyster now prised open often revealed hidden pearls that glistened to the eye. Mostly the issues that surfaced were those of normal adolescence, but extreme anger, frustration and pain were never far away either. Bridging involved listening, teasing out and discussion of issues raised with the occasional giving of advice if requested. This first time verbalising of inner problems seemed to help many cope better. Whether it was a minor or major problem, it was their problem, and they classified it as such. The existence of a confidential sounding board, a listening ear was for some sufficient. Problems outside my capabilities were re-directed to a professional when permitted. In essence the teacher, career counsellor or principal plays the role of a confessor when trusted. Solutions did not always exist but neither were they always sought. I always recalled the request from the patient visiting the doctor, "Cure me of the pain I have." Following examination the medic states, "You have no pain," only for the patient to reply, "Then cure me of the pain I think I have." Bridge building, as thus briefly outlined, is certainly no mysterious science and still many did not appreciate fully the vital role that it can play in the lives of teenagers.

Certainly all this begins to appear like a confessional system. Perhaps the decline in Church practice and outlet for unburdening oneself has contributed much to the stress and isolation of modern youth. The role of a listener must never be under-estimated. Over and over I was convinced that reaching out and spending time was important even if only for a brief ten-minute period in the life of an individual coping with a crisis. Many mini crises were thus defused, preventing a build-up and explosion with possibly more serious consequences. In moments of confrontation with other teachers, it was surprising how difficult pupils found it to extricate themselves from trouble. The simple word 'Sorry', often foreign to their vocabulary, was rarely chosen. It took time for them to accept its importance, even if only half-meant when used, as it got them off the initial hook on which they had stupidly impaled themselves.

Life can't stop, I told them. The clock ticks on. On the spot inquiries over 'Who said what' in class confrontations, like government tribunals took too long. This repeated advice was generally accepted. At least it helped in putting out the early fire. I could never understand how quick students were to take rigid stances on minor matters as it left little room for negotiation. Confrontation seemed at times to be courted without any thought given to how to solve the problem. Youthful impetuosity is a partial explanation, but the cuteness of my school generation was certainly lacking. Were we better able to read teachers and communicate more openly?

Some teachers, horrendous as it sounds, and I was one, looked back in sneaky admiration to the old days when the token two slaps, the quick fix justice of that system resolved minor problems on the spot. In the new enlightened era that approach has been replaced by the slow and protracted form filling, office visitations, endless parental phone calls, warnings, and detentions, suspensions that occasionally finished up with expulsion. Once locked into this system many viewed it as tedious, time consuming and delayed justice, which students and teachers detested. I fully realise that in expressing even a grudging respect for the old discipline one runs the risk of being classified as a possible sadist if not dinosaur. It must also be conceded that no argument can ever justify the barbaric excesses of some who had a 'licence to kill' in the bad old days.

Rarely would I choose to meet a pupil in my office when I knew a serious problem was troubling them, preferring instead to stroll with the pupil around the extensive school fields away from the prying eyes and confining walls. This airy in-step approach facilitated easy conversation where direct eye-to-eye contact across an office table might prove embarrassing or a problem. At other times the casual follow-up silent nod, wink of an eye, word of praise, passing query in a crowded corridor regarding health, sport etc., even the mere turning of a blind eye to minor infringements, ignoring the whiff of cigarette smoke, all were more meaningful and important gestures than the formal conversation. These mini overtures reinforced the bonds of trust and confidence that had taken months to establish. The relationship brought about with such individuals, if not a courtship process could best be described as an unwritten contract. Each participant clearly understood that openness and honesty respected the boundaries, sensitivities and limitations involved in the partnership exercise. Neither side had any hidden agenda, the word ingratiation, licking up to, or patronising never applied. Occasionally the wave of positive discipline that resulted and flowed, removed the flotsam and unnecessary baggage that many carried. After this, progress and possibilities were much greater.

Time and time again in later years pupils who had benefited, even temporarily, from such a policy came back to me. This was sufficient confirmation for me to continue with this strategy. Their smiling eyes and friendly attitude was recognition in itself that neither of our efforts had been wasted. Friendships forged and contacts made lasted long after school time. On a personal level I doubt if they will ever fully understand what this dividend meant to me. Few outside teaching appreciate the vacuum in which a teacher operates. He may be an artist in his own right, but he rarely sees the finished canvas. I had that rare pleasure on many an occasion. The contract now brought into existence as a result of the bridging facilitated the easier transfer of academic knowledge and overall integration of the student at risk, making schooling a more rewarding experience. Inner self-confidence and decreased anxiety led to a positive self-image and self-control on the part of the pupil and was always a more effective and desirable form of discipline than that brought about by imposed rules and regulations, which suffocated and stifled and were in reality a containment policy.

This extra dimension to my teaching life got me over the tedium and boredom of class routine that often sat uneasy with me. The old-fashioned imposed discipline was certainly not the discipline sought by me, as it lacked the warmth, confidence, trust, charity and sense of well-being that the bridging involved since it elevated, respected, opened doors and gave freedom of choice to individuals who needed it most.

If some pupils choose to remember me as a strict, cross country man who ran a tight ship and took few prisoners, there were others with a different tale to tell, though they rarely broke confidentiality. In turn, I also must respect the confessional seal. It is enough to admit that the issues discussed covered the whole range of the human condition.

I trust that this other side of a personality as outlined in this chapter goes some way in redressing the balance in my favour. Like the Janus figure I kept an eye on different shores. One could conclude that too often an academic education is divorced from real feelings and fails to address with sufficient attention the worries and cares of perplexed and troubled minds. There was a complex simplicity involved in the bridging process; I was a fulfilled teacher, secure and confident in the approach taken. In revealing more of myself to this minority who found themselves in the Awkward Squad, they more than anybody knew me best. Working with this ten per cent certainly gave me the greatest satisfaction in teaching.

THE 'CROSS COUNTRY' MAN

"Excuse me Sir, teacher sent me down to mark up the First Year rolls; the class captain is absent after lunch."

With a beaming smile that would open a bank door the pint-sized pupil stood framed in the open office door.

"Good man, step in, there's the roll copy open on the table. What class are you in?"

"Class 127, Sir."

"The biros are there too, on a string, tied to the table leg. Never saw that before – did you?"

"No Sir, it's a good idea."

"This way they never get lost. You know how to enter the roll?"

"Yes Sir – blue above the line, red below for afternoon, isn't that right Sir?"

"You learn fast, well done! Back to class now, thank you!"

"Can I ask one question, Sir?"

"Certainly, ask away."

"That silver cup on the top shelf, Sir? My friend who sits beside me says you are the cross-country teacher, but my brother in Fifth Year says that you are the crossest country teacher with cups to prove it. I don't understand what he means."

"What else did your brother say?"

"That under no circumstances was I to cross you; what do they mean, is it true?"

"Of course it's true, but really, I don't want anyone to know about it, you won't tell anybody will you?"

"No Sir, I promise."

Not for the first time I now entered into this word play game.

"That's the Kingston cup you're looking at up there. Sometimes I give it out to pupils who have success in sport or get very high marks in a project, just for a weekend, to take home as a prize. Nothing to do with the word King in the history books –Kingstons – the shirt shop in

Dublin sponsored that trophy, just like Nike and Umbro would today. Remember now whenever you are very, very proud of something you do you can come right in, and I'll give the cup to you for a short loan. It might be in a few months time, next year or even the year after. When the time comes you will know yourself. Don't forget then to come in and claim it, you will have earned it. It can be our secret and of course your parents too. I call it the 'Gaisce Cup'. That's Irish for a great effort or achievement. Your time will come too. Did your brother ever bring it home?"

"No, I don't think so."

"Well, he has time left too. Don't tell anybody about what I just told you. Off you go now, have I cleared up your questions?"

"Perfectly Sir, thanks, someday I'll come in and want to take it home."

"Good, I know you will. By the way that's how I got the cup too, for being the Crossest Teacher of all and I'm proud of it too, just like you will be."

Cross Country, where do I begin? At various stages in my life different sports took over. Gaelic at all times, hurling too, squash, running, swimming, cycling and in later years walking. Each in turn made its own demands, but cross-country, which I stumbled into, gave more satisfaction than my beloved Gaelic. No, I never achieved anything in games, certainly nothing worthy enough to take home a trophy in the story I conjured up for the perplexed first-year, considering the enjoyment of participating sufficient reward in itself. Other than getting caught up in jogging and Marathon training in the 1980's craze like countless other people, I never ran a race in my life, but that didn't stop me from training. Any real knowledge about athletics was limited in the extreme. Today I can proudly claim that in Kerry I taught Jerry Kiernan, the Olympia marathon runner, along with David Gillick the reigning European sprint champion as a past pupil. No credit however can be claimed, as it was History I taught them. When students referred to me as the Cross Country Teacher, the title, half-deserved, contained a grain of truth more than outsiders fully appreciated.

Take whatever meaning you want as I answered to both over time. Initially the running/jogging club in the college was looked upon as good basic stamina training for all field games, no more no less. Before long this club took on a life on its own in the school, flourished and blossomed in spite of this innocent, haphazard approach. Due credit must be given to the local Dundrum club who trained and polished the raw talent that the school discovered. Many pupils recall the coaxing and bribery adopted by me to make sure the best teams took the field in competitions. The loneliness of the long distance runner is not easily understood; however it was amazing how attractive a half-day in the Phoenix Park was for those wishing to escape class. More I.O.U's for students were cashed than is worth remembering. These running teams down the years brought us no small amount of success. Individuals discovered latent talent for the first time in their lives that required only direction. At whatever level they competed or stage they finished in a race, honest endeavour was rewarded with enjoyment. It was palpable and patent for all to see. I boasted that like a good greyhound person a potential runner could be spotted from a gait or stride taken across the schoolyard. When it did manifest itself I motivated, chased and trained my victim to give running a try. Many did so initially to get me off their backs, but openly admitted later to enjoying the experience. Organization and training were the strong points of my co-conspirators and fellow teachers, both Trojan workers. We worked hand in glove together, considering ourselves fortunate.

Outsiders to the sport must appreciate that in a team of eight, the back runners finishing down the field have a crucial role to play in the overall team result. This fact more than anything else endeared me to the sport. Every runner then had his individual contribution to make. At major championships where every point was vital, those down the field, the back runners, often decided the destiny of the trophy as the scoring system was based on a proportional representational total. This elevated the 'Domestiques' as in the Tour De France, the non- elite competitors in the eyes of all. They were valued accordingly. Those wide smiles of satisfaction witnessed on countless occasions were reward in itself for mentors involved. Laughter is now my reaction on viewing the fading photo of the very first team to represent the college, trailblazers, four young pupils posing in school blazers. Conscripts might best describe them. Fiachra, now a farmer near Mondello winces when he is reminded that he fainted, while another novice vomited violently. Lunchtime chips were blamed on that occasion. I was as proud of them as any team that subsequently ever brought home National Titles to the college. No school colours existed then; like pirates we competed under flags of convenience, white vests, coloured jumpers even cast off "Sloppy Joes" from American parcels that had long failed to fit their recipient fathers. As for running shoes, they were unheard of. Tennis shoes, Blackthorn boots, otherwise bare feet sufficed, punishment in the extreme when the underfoot conditions were muddy and stony.

Those borrowed and pirated hand-me-down colours cut no dash, simply drew attention and trumpeted our arrival to the better-clad rivals in other schools. Sartorial elegance had to wait before we lined out in green and gold O'Neill singlets, and with borrowed spikes we looked the part. If some expressed surprise at the choice of colour, I had the added pleasure of roaring on my county colours for the next thirty years. Looking back over the years faces are recalled, names cascade, events replayed, too many to zoom in on, yet certain incidents and facts do stand out. The impressive cross-country mahogany trophy shields presently on display in the college, fashioned and spoke-shaved in our Woodwork Department, were once planks cobbled together as a last minute makeshift suitcase for one of our former staff returning from Africa. In donating the seasoned timber he recalled a porter running across Lagos airport with the weighty load balanced on his head. As a school we recycled long before it ever became fashionable.

I recall as if it was only yesterday the well-planned victory coup in a Dublin open race with the much-cherished prize of a BBC computer, one of the first seen in our classrooms. Surely a museum piece by now, where it still lies in my attic. Week after week it was loaned out to the runners like a library book. We have indeed come a long way to the modern I-Pod and Blackberry.

The "Event of Events" was still to come with the organised busload of runners who witnessed John Treacy's triumph on the Limerick racecourse in the World Cross Country Championships, in a quagmire of mud. On that day he was our Ronnie Delaney of the Melbourne Olympics. If men cried in ecstasy, the pupils who witnessed were baptised in the sport for life. Imaginations were fired. The Pope in his visit to the same venue years later may have had better weather conditions but I doubt if he matched the excitement of the day. In time no doubt those privileged students will boast they once saw history made by a Waterford man.

Were we ahead of our time when we instructed the shin-splintered athlete, unable to train for a final, to train in the local swimming pool, a non- swimmer hanging on for dear life over a four week period, before ever the classic race horses in Vincent O'Brien's stables were introduced to the same therapy? It worked for us, as did the prayers at Knock by both teams, before and especially after the race, to give thanks for the first silver registered in the All Irelands. We courted help from all sources, and yet year after year the team goal – A National Title - eluded us. Silver and bronze, a handful, but the elusive gold always beyond our reach. I was restless, unfulfilled, even greedy, not on a personal level but rather for the teams and for the School overall who had supported us. Who doesn't want to be a winner, if only for once? Dues had been paid in full; victory was deserved. Brains were wracked; something was missing. In desperation a strategy was devised; home advantage might give us the edge. This psychological advantage was for many a figment of a sportsman's imagination. Still it was worth trying if only to rid it from the equation as a possible solution. All other bases we had covered; strategy, talent, coaches, enthusiasm and experience hard earned, without the desired result.

Sport is sport but the politics of sport is a very strange animal indeed. In desperation we forwarded our home grounds as the venue for the Dublin, Leinster and All Ireland finals in turn. As a running venue it had few equals. It was accepted, but it imposed a heavy workload, not to mention responsibility on the school organisers. Perennial bureaucrats on national committees who run sports are a breed apart, best avoided lest contamination takes place. While such committees are essential, invariably each member has his own agenda and guards care-

fully his specific power base. Jealousies abound as each jostles for the
limelight. Devious and cynical, especially to outsiders, they could advise Machiavelli and teach Masonic Lodges a thing or two. I vowed always to give such folk a wide berth, and now here we were working
hand in glove with a nest of organising vipers. There was always a consolation in the possibility that it might give our athletes the edge so we
suffered silently, forever conscious that the myriad of jobs in organising
an event for over one thousand runners on three separate dates might
overwhelm and distract us from our main objective, training and ultimate victory. What Groucho Marx said about clubs, applies equally to
committees: "I would never join any club that would have me as a
member."

Final day, having qualified in the preliminaries, saw me perched on
the long gone high pillars of the bridge that now straddles the Luas at
Balalley, animated, excited, bellowing in an encouraging voice that carried all the way up the grassy gallops, our secret weapon, the three-
hundred-yard punishing climb. Lucky for me video cameras were then
a rare and expensive item. Athletes still say they can hear my roar in
their ears; in jest they claim that they were too afraid to stop had they
needed to. Let it be recorded that the home advantage worked the or-
acle. We knew every bump, hollow and blade of grass on that Calvary
Hill where we nailed the opposition round after round. Our athletes,
heroes all, were champions of Ireland at last!

Celebration was farthest from my thoughts. In moments of absolute
bliss such as this, rare indeed, my normal extrovert personality closes
down and I retire totally into my shell, silently savouring the joy of the
occasion. Nobody could take this title from us; it was won on merit
and it was ours. An inner voice said 'Walk Easy,' no gloating. What
was it the child said about the Pope's visit to the Phoenix Park? Everybody celebrated except his father, a grounds man, who had to pick up
the accumulated rubbish and bottles for weeks after. It was a similar
story for us organisers as the four toilets in the First Year corridor were
blocked and over flowing when the crowds departed. I was good
enough to be my own servant; nobody else could be expected to do
such dirty work. Consequently, sleeves were rolled up, stench ignored,

a guaranteed dose of reality to bring a person down from the clouds. A small price indeed to pay for what was possibly the happiest day, certainly in my sporting life, if not teaching career.

As a postscript one minor matter needs explanation. We had delayed naming the last member of the official team until ten minutes before the race, in the interests of team morale. We wished to disappoint nobody. Any one of the seven remaining members of the large panel of fourteen, all fully fit, deserved the last position and honour of representing the college at this highest level. Like the others they too were loyal and cherished but destined to sit it out on the subs bench. They anxiously awaited the draw from the hat made minutes before the off. It was a tough call for any manager. In the interest of fairness and transparency seven papers were placed in a hat, for the selection that took place in their presence. The lucky winner was applauded on nomination. Justice had been done or more importantly it had been seen to be done—or so they thought!

Clarification however is now necessary and long overdue. If seven pieces of paper went into that hat there was but a single name, my nominee. Nothing was left to chance. The vote was rigged, Mugabe style. I had made my choice on merit, unity and morale was extended to the subs' bench. It has to be admitted that in doing so I was betraying the trust of a co–manager and possibly the very pupils for whom I involved myself in the sport in the first instance. I had waited too many years to let the opportunity go by. The nagging voice in my head shouting 'Foul Play,' it was ignored hypnotised as I was by the glint of gold. Apologies, long overdue, are extended now to this successful team from a distance of some twenty years. Shortly before retiring, guilt-ridden I appraised my co–manager of the foul deed done. I dreaded losing a friend for life but my apology was quickly accepted. It was after all the measure of the man.

I retained contact with games right throughout my teaching career; even when the flesh was weak the spirit was strong. Few teams managed to take to the field without my sideline support, invited or not by their managers. No one should ever underestimate the view obtained of the playing fields from the upstairs classrooms, especially on Friday afternoons. If I absented myself from supporting my goalkeeping son, I still witnessed him from afar saving the day in a Gaelic penalty shootout. It was as much as my nerves would allow. Enthusiasm has on occasions to be curbed. The last thing he would have wanted was a raving, roaring father supporting him from the sidelines. This was an affliction visited on all other sportsmen I had contact with across the years.

HUMOUR

Once when a parent innocently asked me if humour had a place or role in the classroom, I surprised him with an enthusiastic reply, "You better believe it, although at times it should carry a health warning!" Few, if any, of the teacher's manuals recommend it, as paradoxically it can be explosive and destructive, even boring in the wrong hands, but equally a wonderful and imaginative weapon in the arsenal of the teacher who engages with it. Like dynamite it must be handled with care. I always cherished and valued the importance of laughter as a safety valve in defusing tension in the boiler-house atmosphere of a classroom. Over years the vein of comedy in individuals or situations was mined and while the mother lode was never found there existed enough scattered nuggets to encourage me to continue. In truth I was duly rewarded, enriched and educated in my quest and must show restraint in not wandering off or free wheeling on numerous anecdotes and stories that pepper most teachers' lives.

Before venturing out I proffer a few words of wisdom and advice to any would-be classroom comedian. Know yourself and know your audience. While humour and comedy give full reign to the idiosyncratic, zany and unpredictable side of one's personality, the teacher must never abuse the position he has in class by acting as court jester. I knew my own limitations and ability whenever I facilitated, encouraged and cultivated the emergence of laughter. Any comical streak and latent talent had at best to be tapped into and held in tight rein. Genuine humour in the classroom has to be a two way street. As on stage, timing is of the essence, otherwise it can be a recipe for chaos and disaster. When my authoritarian mask occasionally slipped and revealed a hidden unknown side, it was intentional. I took frivolity seriously. If laughing at my own expense I was in control. Junior students were off-limits and spared this insight, but in the presence of senior students I was myself. It was a futile to attempt to conceal or pretend in the presence of such perceptive individuals. Invariably the daily progress of the academic work at the blackboard facilitated such time-out moments and flights of fancy and not just by me alone. The pupils in turn warmed to such temporary distractions and rarely missed the opportunity of giving a fair wind to the balloon when it was airborne.

I never underestimated the importance of such occasions, however momentary and impromptu they were in distracting and enlivening the monotony of class routine. When dark clouds of tension lingered on the class horizon they were regularly diffused and dissipated in a thunderclap of laughter. Class interruptions, microphone announcements, facial expressions, poses struck, text references, window-trapped wasps, together with the ever present seagulls and crows in the playground were all potential sparks to ignite, curtain calls in themselves to be ignored or taken advantage of. Brief as performances were, they were responsible in confirming for delighted pupils the strongly held belief that their teacher, 'full of capernocity and function' who stood before them, was indeed a little odd. Behaving in such manner no doubt provided enough proof that would stand up in any court of law. I never did regret meddling with humour on this makeshift stage. One learned quickly to read the frown of boredom and the glint of entertainment on the faces of the listening audience.

Follow me out of the classroom, down the long corridor, after a strenuous class; exhausted, blood pressure soaring, having 'chawed out' and failed gloriously to motivate yet another intelligent if lazy pupil, whispering, tomorrow he might be won over. My enthusiasm for Davitt and Parnell's New Departure scarcely dented his curiosity levels. He was happy in his blanket of bored apathy: how dare I intrude? The perplexed student didn't know whether he was supposed to cry or to laugh as my words of censure went over his head, as did the few token words of praise thrown in his direction as I exited the room. A vain effort on my part in sugaring the pill and lessening the tension created. Concerned and frustrated at my own limitations I patrolled the crowded corridor only to be halted and side tracked en route by the acrid whiff of sulphur that pulsed the nostrils in passing. This glorious distraction and invitation, which could never be resisted, provided me with an opportunity to perform in my favoured venue, none other than the Sixth Year toilets. With a dramatic entrance and warning shout of 'Show time, Gentlemen,' a quick turn is made into this offside precinct in a raid that would do credit to a Bronx drugs bust. In today's world a similar action by a teacher would require a warrant, signed in triplicate by the Board of Management, together with a posse of independent witnesses to vouch for one's actions if not for one's overall character in the first place.

The 'Sketch' student-warning cry, somewhat late, still gave time for startled smokers within to react instantly, distancing themselves from the discarded butts that littered the terrazzo floor. Pavlov the scientist would have been proud of this instinctive response. For those special accomplices the drill that followed was well known; admit, unload, token fine, quick exit, case closed, an 'easy cop' in school lingo. The hard case addicted smoker or uninitiated novice often brazen and reluctant to come clean had to watch in horror as, magician like, I pickpocketed from secreted locations the contraband cigarettes and lighters, before proceeding, hands aloft in full view of all, to the accompaniment of cheers and groans of 'Scab' and 'Meanie,' to bend, and slowly break a single token offending fag prefaced by a 'spiel'.
'Breathalyser, now, ' with nose inched closer to tightly closed lips lest they betray.
'Deep breath. That's it, in all the way. Don't be afraid. No wheeze. Good man. Hold it. One, two, three – exhale. Stand back gentlemen, from the dragon flames.'
'Caught. Guilty. Red handed. Don't lie,' the staccato words rifled the air.
'Not me, Sir. I don't smoke. Look at my hands, no stains.'
The puff may have been invisible but the blast and pong from the ' bronicals 'always betrayed. The flushed faces were condemned on the spot with flimsy yet conclusive evidence beyond which there was no appeal. In fairness I never destroyed more than two cigarettes, dramatic and entertaining as the gesture was for the now crowded area following an invasion of First Years from the excited corridor who were my real target audience. It would have been torture in the extreme to exceed this number, as the culprit would have to witness valuable and hard-earned pocket money flushed down the toilet.

This regular routine of mine was not without purpose, since many of the younger pupils, agog, were witnessing for the first time. This helped to bolster an image, especially when they later added to the story in telling for those not privileged in the first instance. Call this image making and spin. The illusion was always maintained by the senior pupils, who if caught played along to the gawking gallery. They over time learned to discreetly palm back, unobserved, the confiscated items that I held unseen behind my back as the rant and rage continued for effect. At this stage two audiences were present, those gathered in who stood before me excited and distracted by the hullaballoo in the toilets, and those behind who knew the score and had been coached in pulling off the regular charade. It rarely failed to entertain. The occasional mock argument and cry of ' But SIR' only added to the occasion. The culprits knew that all 'goods' could be redeemed from the shoebox behind my office door later in the day, once the token charitable donation had been paid to the school secretary. This money was always accounted for at the end of the year when the main contributors approved of its deserving target. On one such occasion it financed the medical expenses of the hardened smoker who desired to be cured of his addiction. When the medical earring implants and patch solution failed gloriously, he was exempted from all future fines. I know for sure that my accomplices got as much enjoyment out of these regular performances as I did. No senior ever queried my actions; they just accepted it as entertainment, a worthwhile distraction in the busy day of a normally abnormal teacher.

Journey resumed, gown billowing, I abandon that stage and continued my journey in the direction of a favourite and cherished haunt, the Woodwork Room. The Sawdust Café, where all my free class periods were spent, a sanctuary and haven ruled over by two teaching colleagues, craftsmen and co-conspirators in drama, where another equally attractive sideshow was played out daily. I can never fully explain the transformation that came over me on entering this independent republic, membership of which was confined to a very select vestry of three people. Two other applicants, understudies, waited patiently in the wings for Equity cards, conscious that they were unlikely to be called upon. In such surroundings over thirty-five years I served my time in a comic goon routine that went mostly unscripted. On entry, if class was in progress, on cue the lean Kerryman teaching at the blackboard would halt proceedings, hand me the sweeping brush and with a flourishing gesture in a loud voice issue orders that the room be swept, now that the sawdust and shavings had once more accumulated to the annoyance of all. Much to the amazement of the bemused pupils I would oblige without uttering a word.

In my role as servant boy, the brown overalls were donned, an open acknowledgement that the now discarded black cloak of authority carried little influence in this department. Duly instructed, with the class in progress, I swept between the workbenches where pupils struggled and mastered mortised joints on imaginative examination projects. Either that, or a pupil reprimanded earlier by me, still bearing a grudge, would take pleasure behind my back in discreetly pushing further deposits of sawdust and shavings onto the floor I had already swept. The trap sprung would result in a sharp reprimand by my 'ganger' at the blackboard. In false humility, head bowed, I would retrace my steps, mumbling an apology, and repeat the sweeping. What the pupils made of these antics we never asked, we just enjoyed it. A role reversal since now one tasted medicine so liberally dispensed in my own fiefdom further up the corridor. Juniors were agog and amused year after year by this submissive role and unusual behaviour. Gradually pupils accepted me as part of the furniture, the" blockhead" in the joinery shop, seasoned certainly, wood wormed a little but nevertheless accepted, to the point of being finally ignored.

This I took as the supreme compliment, as conversations overheard while sweeping concerning weekend parties and lady friends took place in my presence, as if I did not exist. I respected this confidentiality and as a teacher was ever envious of the informality, lax discipline and teaching atmosphere that prevailed in those special rooms. Trust, approachability and friendship between teacher and pupil was the norm here, in truth a promised land one could only dream about yet never conjure up in my own structured and formal classes. This was a bridge, a ladder, even a dramatic stage in the educational process that I stumbled on accidentally and wished to remain on, as it afforded me an opportunity to praise, observe and appreciate the skills, dexterity and craftsmanship of talented individuals that went unnoticed and ignored in my own formal education. Moreover it forged relationships and bonds that would have been impossible elsewhere in the school.

To the untutored eye one might have thought I was wasting my time in this Academy. Nothing was further from the truth. As a late entrant I appreciated the skills and hours spent there, and when occasionally approaching the lunchtime bell a forward student drew attention to the unwashed dishes in the kitchen sink, on cue the other 'Sergeant' would throw a tea towel in my direction barking orders that they be washed quickly lest my membership of the select club be cancelled. If I was lingering in their midst it was in the hope that the extensive knowledge of my chosen tutors might in some inexplicable way rub off on me. Minutes later, classes dismissed behind closed doors, all three comedians had difficulty in restraining ourselves from side-splitting laughter, boasting that the impromptu script had been acted out successfully yet again for another appreciative student audience. There was no need for stress-busting tablets with such daily diversions. The child in each of us emerged and played as of old. Who said that Óisín was the only visitor to Tír na nÓg?

It was my opinion that many or most teachers took themselves and their duties far too seriously. I saw to it that the same certainly could never be said about me. Regretfully teachers are too often passive observers of humanity and humour. The role of an active participant and instigator was my preferred option. 'Stir it up,' my colleague would demand if silence reigned on the empty first year corridor outside the café. Rarely did I need a second invitation. 'Coast clear' was the signal for me to step outside and commence roaring at the non-existent passing pupil. Admonitions and reprimands boomed and echoed, shattering the school tranquillity, 'Get out you pup,' 'Second time today. Office,' as further up the corridor within earshot behind classroom doors innocent souls shivered, pitying the lamb up for slaughter. Imaginations ran riot. More than anything else these brief performances marked out the fact that the roaring individual was not a person to be trifled with, and best avoided if at all possible. Occasionally sympathetic teachers would often peer out in vain to identify, if not to rescue, the offending pupil. It was a bonus when they later advised me in the privacy of the staff room that such pupils were not worth getting a heart attack over. Straight-faced I apologised for interrupting classes and assaulting their sensitive ears. Devilment is the only word to describe best such antics. Only once ever did a startled innocent smoker materialise from the toilets to witness the charade in progress. I can still see his questioning eye and double take as he scanned the long vacant corridor. Sympathy more than shock was his main reaction. When this happened I vented my last few words in his direction before retreating again into the safety of the Woodwork Room where the real adult 'trouble makers' attempted to regain composure for the upcoming class. We like many other people abhorred vacuums; we convinced ourselves that it was our duty to fill them.

In the wrong hands attempted humour can have dangerous consequences. When used there must be strict rules of engagement. No wounding, cynical, cheap, and personal or downgrading comments can be allowed. Humour in the classroom must never be equated with simple joke making. When employed it should never be a one-way traffic system or solo performance orchestrated by a teacher. It must be stressed that the power and position of the teacher can be abused when it is assumed a captive audience exists. Independent-minded individuals existed in all classes who if given half the chance might blossom when encouraged. Cheek is not to be confused with being forward; the glint in the eye is a precious commodity to be nurtured as it often indicates a carefree spirit who has a wide grasp of humanity. Such fortunate individuals, if elevated, possess 'give and take', understanding, generosity of spirit and disarming smiles. Pushed forward by the group they often emerge as spokesmen. When the hard call has to be made they maintain their independence. Academic ability does not always come into the question. It is directly through these characters that class humour can be channelled. Their presence I valued and sought, and surprisingly they were not as rare as I initially thought. The annual musicals performed by Transition Year students tapped into this vein with miraculous results. The transformation in character afforded by the footlights was unbelievable. A few I directed into amateur dramatics, as they could swan their routine on any boards. I thank and classify them as equal partners in the humour equation, which like a spirit level helped keep the equilibrium in the teaching day.

What do you say to the chirpy fifteen-year-old who sidles up to you in class on foot of repeated incidents of minor pilfering within their group? My best efforts in appealing to the seventh commandment were futile. 'Mr.Mac – might I suggest you take a break for five minutes, have a cup of tea and leave us on our own?' Honest, if blunt, I complied with this unusual request but stayed within earshot in the interests of safety on the corridor outside. Loud murmurings followed, excited chatter, the banging of desks, all could be heard behind the closed door beyond which I waited nervously. Finally the summons from the craning head, 'You can come in now, Sir.' There on the table was the missing money and lost pen, together with a pair of shoes and stockings. I knew better than to ask questions, and resumed teaching. Rough justice had been administered. There was no need to leave the blackboard to discover who the shoeless 'Joe' was. The scarlet-faced individual hugging the back seat did not have to be verbally identified. A valuable lesson in life had been taught, and not by me. A serious situation had been defused. I still chuckle, as this was only to be the start of a wonderfully humorous relationship with a very special group of individuals.

As always I was a sucker for the repeated punch line or cliché in class. 'Treat people properly.' 'Keep your word.' ' Do unto others.' Humour seemed to surround me and emerged from the most unlikely quarters. The thud of an apple that burst against the windowpane is recalled, as I was finishing up a class well beyond the bell at break time. Enraged, and abandoning my perch in an upstairs classroom, I swooped on a playground mêlée, sinking my talons into the neck of the guilty party; judge, jury and executioner in fifteen seconds flat. A record diffusion, detention called, problem solved. With smug satisfaction I resumed my teaching only to have the traumatised pupil recover his voice thirty minutes later when he brazenly interrupted my class, informing me in a loud voice that his friend had owned up and admitted his guilt to the Principal. Embarrassed, I apologised to the innocent victim in front of the bemused pupils and in reparation I wrote out an I.O.U cheque, a monopoly like card to get-out-of-jail, which could be cashed in the next time he found himself in real trouble. Satisfied, he graciously accepted my offer. Surprise is a very inadequate word to express a reaction when the same party, before the day was out, knocked again on my door insisting I honour immediate payment, as he now wished to collect on his debt. I squared matters, but never told him that it cost me dearly – three supervision classes for the irate offended teacher who had the rare pleasure of teaching this scholar. Don't talk about leading with the chin! I could only laugh along with the overjoyed pupils who witnessed my humiliation. The sucker punch had landed, a technical K.O. A promise was a promise. I practised what I preached. These are just instances of the humour that I regularly looked forward to and was rewarded by in the classroom. However, they pale into insignificance when I recall a high-spirited class, disruptive in the eyes of many, who more than all the others taught me important lessons never to be forgotten. Friday afternoon in their company was wonderfully challenging as the smell of cordite always greeted the incoming teacher. This was the supreme test; succeed here and you deserved, so to speak, to be called a teacher. I refused to lower my sights or accept the less than complimentary epithets used by others in describing them. Rival groups vied with each other and the teacher for control of the steering wheel. The destination ultimately arrived at was not always the desired one; neither was the circuitous round the houses route. In this electric atmosphere the challenge was taken up but not before appreciating that it was their differences that had to be celebrated.

There, in their midst, sat Albert hugging the wall, aloof, introverted, observing all with a detached suspicious piercing eye. When addressed or invited to participate, he eventually whispered in an inaudible voice only to quickly curl up again into his solitary shell. The class conscience, give credit where it is due, like protective crows rallied around the wounded one. Clearly defined markers, warning signposts, announced that Albert was 'off limits' to all with bullying tendencies, teachers included. He was a protected species, treasured by all.

To ignore Albert would have gone against my principles. The limited homework he presented was well up to standard and he was praised accordingly. I treaded cautiously and before long my initial advances and probes were sanctioned by Albert's self-appointed minder who 'allowed' me to talk with Albert in the privacy of my office. Such approval was given only after a protracted courtship. This was registered as a breakthrough. However, the monosyllabic words I extracted from Albert across the fragile bridge, 'Yes,' 'No,' and the oft-repeated whisper 'Maybe tomorrow,' certainly did not enlighten him or me. No progress was reported. Contented and self-sufficient in his own silent world made him an ideal candidate for any Trappist Monastery. He sat there, staring at me with a disarming smile. Over months I failed to touch base with him or reveal the personality within. The simple physical exercises recommended in an effort to coax him to uncurl his stooped posture and strange gait, unseen in my office, similarly failed. With patience exhausted over weeks, I welcomed the advice of his minder who took me aside saying, 'Give it up, Mr .Mac. Accept him as different, just as we do.' With this 'out of the mouths of babes' wisdom I reluctantly raised my siege, somewhat deflated. He was indeed a locked personality beyond my reach. This was one of the rare moments in my career when defeat was admitted.

The educational system duly processed him over the five long years he remained with us. His success in examinations was a consolation and tribute to those patient teachers who assisted him. Finally he left with our prayers and blessings, though we were concerned for his future in the larger world outside. The responsibility of reaching out to such an individual, who I refused to categorise in all charity, weighed heavily with me. It was Ghandi who preached that we must be the change we wished to see in the world. In Albert's case, I had wished to be that difference. In failing, consolation came in the knowledge that my best was not good enough.

No, the story does not end there. Fast-forward another five years. The venue: the Sawdust Café, lunch break. The occasional flying visits by past pupils who called in to pay respects to former teachers were welcomed and appreciated. I have queried their reasons in doing so elsewhere in this memoir, curiosity, trumpeting success, confronting past demons, who knows. Now another tall, erect, well-dressed, trimmed moustached individual who launched himself into our room, confidently saluting us by name days before Christmas, certainly created an impression as we struggled to put a name to the face. Eventually, somewhat bemused, he had to re-introduce himself. 'Albert. Albert,' he repeated, now annoyed. 'Don't you remember me?' Rooted to our lunchtime chairs, suspiciously and with incredulity, our genuine surprise was only surpassed by warm greetings a moment later. Perhaps we had not failed after all. Gainfully employed he was now enjoying life to the full; the clouded diamond sparkled. Our polite chitchat in that short break never went deep and as he headed for the door, waving goodbye, I plucked up courage to go after him.

It was difficult to associate the two personalities, the old and the new, in the same breath. Curiosity emboldened me. Drawing him aside quietly I asked but a single question. It was either that or remain mystified for the rest of my life. 'Please tell me where the old Albert went to?' Grinning ear to ear he whispered, 'He never existed.' 'What?' I gasped in disbelief.

The act, the pose struck, the mask worn over all the years was, he admitted with a wry smile, simply a survival strategy adopted within hours of entry on his very first day into the secondary system with the sole purpose of deflecting attention from himself. 'Did I ever hand up homework? No,' he proudly confessed, rephrase that: boasted is a better word. 'Was I bullied? Who would have dared? Teachers gave up on me quickly. I had a free ride the full five years. Nobody really bothered with me, all except yourself, you lasted the longest. There were times when I thought you had twigged me. Why wouldn't I keep it up with a guaranteed protection policy thrown in?' His eyes danced as he spoke. Dumbfounded, speechless, and incredulous I roared out laughing and congratulated him for such a sustained Oscar performance reminiscent of Hoffmann's Rainman. Not only had I been taken to the cleaners but hung out to dry by an expert. In conscience he began to apologise, but I cut him short and prevented him, saying that it was a privilege to be on the receiving end of such a sting operation. Living as he did five miles from the school location, and close to the city centre, successfully facilitated this double existence. Before he closed the door behind him, stopping on the threshold, one leg in, one leg out, he turned full circle and like magic donned again the mask of the old Albert I knew in the long ago, whispering slowly, 'Say goodbye to me for the last time,' before instantly switching back again. I stood there mesmerised, transfixed and in awe at what he had managed to pull off. 'Do you like my new walk, Mr.Mac? You should, I based it on yours.' As suddenly as he had entered, he walked out of my life forever.

From this distance Albert, I take my hat off to you. You gave me a new insight into humour, and to think the Department of Education paid me to teach a pupil such as yourself. A simple plea I make, Albert? Any possibility you would pay me one very last visit in retirement, just to keep an old man happy before he meets his Maker and applauds Him for giving us a character like yourself. If your one time generous protector was, like me, unaware of the deception I suggest to him that we both stand up and applaud a real artist at work. Yes, I mined the rich vein of humour wherever I found it totally unaware of the fact that I too had been shafted and undermined. And what a pleasure it was.

ICARUS

When during that last hurrah class a most awkward and potentially embarrassing question was asked of me, I avoided it. It hung in the air, teasing and probing, begging to be answered. "What was the greatest disappointment in your teaching career, Mr. Mac?" Unrealised ambition was the answer I could not bring myself to utter. If I lied there and then, few noticed it. Dissimulation is a term I prefer. It was too sensitive an issue for me to reply to honestly. This was neither the time nor the place to face up to certain facts and in the process expose a healing wound. In the best tradition of politicians put on the spot, after a long silent pause, the question was laughed off with an impromptu quip about Kerry's fiasco in not winning the five in a row football titles, quickly adding that the failure of the school Gaelic team to win a National Title or any former pupil to strike real gold with the Dubs were just as disappointing. My references to the tantalising so-near-and-yet-so-far games distracted the audience sufficiently. The ploy got me off the hook as other less serious matters were discussed, sidetracking and parking the tantalising awkward question for another day.

And yet my conscience nagged. Now years later, I still agonise as to whether or not I should address the issue here in an open and honest way. For reasons that will be obvious, it is difficult to broach the topic as it strikes a raw nerve that still twitches involuntarily. My students were weary from hearing my chant that 'talk is cheap'. After all, in a profession in which I was paid to talk, with the implied assumption that what is uttered is reasonably informative and rational, nothing was further from the truth in respect of this issue. With the exception of very close friends I have never opened up on the issue of disappointment, preferring instead to keep it buried deep 'in pectore', as it does not reflect well on my own personality in coping with the stresses and strains that must be endured in any normal life time. In a discussion of this important issue objectivity can never be achieved. Honesty is the best that can be hoped for; it is after all a personal account of events. And yet I had spent a lifetime in History classes pointing out the dangers and pitfalls inherent in any subjective account where emotions run deep.

Now older, battle-scarred, and wiser, I am able to root out and evict from the dark corners of my psyche the disappointment and difficulties that were fed irrationally for too long a period. Each of us has his own demons to face up to; at times we may trivialise, even laugh at other people's fears. In this respect I am no different than anybody else. It is never easy to step outside ones self and unveil the mirror. It all takes time and if the process is a painful one, often a healing may be the result. Disappointment has many names; defeat, disillusionment, despair and occasionally depression. Confession, it is said, is good for the soul but it must be appreciated that what is good in private confession may not be as comforting in public. And yet there is nothing very unusual or remarkable in my story. If it was a breaking point for me, a bridge too far, a fire, that instead of steeling me melted me, at this safe remove I now believe I emerged a better and stronger person at the end of it all. After all, the greatest difficulty with conflict or trouble isn't remembering it, but forgetting it. Thankfully somewhere along the line I have at last forgotten how to remember.

The disappointment referred to concerns a long held ambition of promotion, or more accurately an application for the post of Vice Principal when a position was available in the school. "Is that all?" After such a big build up, one should apologise for mentioning such a mundane and trivial matter, a typical example of the mountain labouring and giving birth to a mouse. Kerry verbosity at its best, what else did you expect? Allow me to elaborate and explain myself more fully. After thirty-seven years teaching, aspiring to such a lofty position was for me no small ambition. It is all too easy for others, particularly outsiders, to minimize another man's dream. Idealists, and I label myself as one, often dream about power centres wherein there are possibilities to extend one's influence, to be a mover and shaker, as current language puts it. To balance the equation I quickly claim that pragmatism and hard graft were not foreign to me at any stage of my career. Some people are happy to cast ideas out in the hope that they will germinate, others seek positions of authority from which possibilities are greater.

Idealism and pragmatism can go hand in hand and are not mutually exclusive.

In the Ireland of the 80's the vocation crisis in religious orders reached its height and as a consequence the teaching orders were forced to introduce Lay Principalships in the overall management of schools. The ever-dwindling numbers of brothers and nuns on the ground brought this decision to a head quicker than many had anticipated in our school. When such a position was advertised I decided in all wisdom not to apply believing that a more worthwhile contribution as a Vice-Principal could be made, if and when the post became available within the school. The De La Salle authorities were notified of my intentions, as I did not want to be seen as lacking ambition. My notification was duly acknowledged and noted in a letter of reply. In retrospect this may have been naïve on my part, a mistake possibly, similar to showing a hand too soon in any political poker game that might logically be expected to follow on such a position becoming vacant. In the years that followed I waited patiently, ambitions undiminished.

In a lifetime of teaching very few opportunities for promotion present themselves and I was flattered that twice I had been approached by outside schools to apply for Vice Principalships in the Dublin area. Head hunting and team building is the expression in the Celtic Tiger that best describes such overtures. I politely declined and thanked those involved for the recognition that the requests implied, on the grounds that my loyalty was and would always be to my own expanding college base. Loyalty for me was of great importance and always came before promotion and self-interest. I will not deny that the transfer market was tempting, especially to a family man with a heavy mortgage and four growing children facing University. I never regretted this personal stance even if it was not fully understood by those who came calling in a world where old-fashioned loyalty had lost much of its meaning. I, after all, had only myself to answer to.

Consequently when the opportunity for Vice-Principal promotion presented itself in the college in 2003, after thirty-seven years teaching, like others my hat was in the ring for a position in the educational boardroom. It certainly was not a decision taken lightly. If anything it was the height of my ambition, as over a lifetime I too dreamed dreams. I certainly knew my limitations, and the possibility that the position would still allow some teaching contact was important, contented as I was in the classroom. At all times I believed I had more to offer and further challenges to meet. All the wise heads predicted that the appointment would be from within the existing staff, as the Principal's post had been filled from the outside transfer market as expected some years previously. Internal promotion such as this within the school was rare, generally only after death or retirement. The criteria for such a selection and promotion had traditionally been seniority, number of years served within the school, a long standing Union position which thankfully was changed in negotiations between the Partners in Education - Teachers, Unions, and the Department and Religious Orders in the mid 90's. This decision was warmly welcomed by me, and voted for at Union level, even though as a senior teacher I might have been expected to vote otherwise. Shades of a turkey voting for Christmas! Seniority per se, all other things being equal, is fine but meritocracy based on ability must override all in the interests of equity and progress. Confident that my long record in the school would withstand analysis, I faced into an interview with the sentiments that the best man should win.

History recalls the dire warnings in Caesar about the Ides of March; had I too failed to grasp the fact that on the very minute I handed over my application in the Secretary's office an excited teacher burst in with the breaking news concerning the Twin Towers bombing in America? '9-11' for me on this side of the Atlantic carries other connotations less significant. Following the interview, the result was made known to me privately some days later via a twenty-second phone call to my home at night informing me that another candidate had been successful. The conversation was short and brief. I put the best skin on the disappointment and continued my bookwork for some hours before finally telling my wife. Before long the reality and impact shook and shattered the foundations of my own personal edifice. I dared to allow myself dream like Icarus only to be disappointed and fall to earth. The walls of my small world remained intact but serious cracks appeared, visible only to me. The new Vice Principal was a past pupil of my own, much younger than I, with legitimate ambitions and credits in his own right. I still recall some twenty years previously calling to his home in early September, and convincing him that he should reject the Civil Service Junior-Ex position he had been offered in that morning's post, on the grounds that I believed he had much more to offer as a teacher in his own school. I had headhunted a talented former scholar and footballer who' over the years in class had confirmed initial judgements. There and then some twenty years later in the privacy of my own office following the official announcement I congratulated him on his nomination as the new Vice-Principal and sincerely wished him well in the days ahead, to clear the ground lest any jealous weeds might take root. Moreover I guaranteed my loyalty and friendship, refusing ever to allow the issue of promotion to come between us. Inwardly if I was shattered, I tried never to let it show.

The unusual aspect of the whole situation, looking back, is that within hours of my own interview, I had penned a letter of thanks to my acting referee in the Order, predicting that I had not been successful. The tone and line of questioning in my interview indicated this very clearly. "In the event of a past pupil, a much younger man getting the appointment, what would your reaction be, Mr. McMahon?" Naïve, possibly innocent, never having submitted to an interview before, I replied honestly and still do not regret the answer given, in pledging loyalty in the event of his success, considering him a worthy candidate. How else could I have answered? Integrity and being true to myself was all important. The importance of this question, and of my refusal to play games, was instantly clear to me on leaving the interview venue. My instincts had never left me down before and I can only suppose that my letter was a vain effort to soften the impact of the official result when it came. This letter I posted from the G.P.O. in O'Connell Street the day after the interview as the cortege and ceremony, en route to Glasnevin cemetery, for the re-internment of Kevin Barry and others buried in Mountjoy, passed by. Historic occasions were always honoured and attended by me, however heavy the heart.

By now I was beginning to think History was haunting me. While I had indeed correctly read the writing on the wall, or should that be in the stars, this follow-up letter was at most a salve to a bruised soul. Had I been naïve in my expectations, in my flight of fancy from the very beginning, fooling myself? Ought I have set boundaries on my ambitions, even curtailed my imagination? "Bullock's notions of an old man dreaming," was how another might have put it more bluntly. Whatever questions remained, privately I like to think it was age that came against me. Nothing to do but get on with life, and finish out the remaining years in the standard harness of teaching.

As with Icarus and soaring ambition, either that or a propensity to over-reach, I was forced to come back down to earth with a bang. It was poor consolation to think that the ancient gods destroyed their favourites first with arrogance, and then with madness. A close Anam Chara supported me in my initial ambitious application yet secretly wanted me to refuse it if successful. He knew me only too well. At home my wife hoped I would not apply in the first instance lest I would exhaust myself in the process if successful. In the telling of this account I have exposed a wound that left a scar, a major one, that does not bear comparison with the serious problems of health and life with which others are often afflicted and tormented. It was what it was; and it was natural to feel bruised and chastened.

Now that all the clouds have passed, life has been good to me. The rewards in finally coming to terms with disappointment can be slow in coming but come they do. Integrity and honour are still intact. Had I been successful in my application, reluctantly admitting to being a workaholic, there always remains the fact that given the demands of the job I might have pushed myself to the point of exhaustion. My father's persistent advice of years past is now fully understood. "Remember you can give students your all, but you cannot and should not bleed for them." How is it that when we get older we can always see the wisdom of advice? Perhaps looking back it is only now that the silver lining becomes visible; who knows a favour may have been done for me, as having retired early I can now appreciate and savour in cold January the snow caps of the high Alps with the prospect of a sun-drenched Tenerife to follow on its heels. If this is the reward for a bruised and fragile ego, it is welcomed.

Ironically it was a philosophical book by a Belfast writer Johnson that enabled me finally to come to terms with the vagaries of life, calming the body and forcing me to take stock. The profound thoughts of philosopher John Moriarty – a humble gentle giant and genius from my home area had yet to be discovered and appreciated. His thoughts have reinforced a willingness to accept, routing in the process the bitter taste that lingered. Nevertheless there still remains an awkwardness in the writing of this account because there is a tendency to live in one's own thoughts. Doubts still linger. Would I have lived contented had I ignored my ambition? Surely it is better to try and fail, rather than fail to try? If the question lingers unanswered in the air on occasions it is now of minor importance. It is easier to accept that one did not attain high office, than to have others question constantly, if successful, why one even applied in the first place. The whole episode was traumatic, even life-changing. It certainly forced me into getting to know myself better however long a time it took for rational acceptance to overcome the emotion of disappointment. We are all tested in life and the hope is that we will emerge wiser for the experience, a better person. Time and reading helped to banish the pain and extract the thorn. Refuge was also often sought in prayer, a most unfashionable concept in today's world. Like medication bought over the counter, progress can be reported by continuous application, or should that be supplication. If nothing else, it teaches you humility and how to count one's blessings. Was it not Calvin that stated, 'We are but actors on a stage with God as an audience'? Religion can be an opium, anaesthetic, refuge even cop-out to the problems of life. Each man to his own.

Alas however, like a lot of self-prescribed balm there was a fly in the ointment. There is no accounting for the unexpected. In an effort to cope with the initial frustration and disappointment, I foolishly launched myself onto Spain's highest mountain, Mount Teide in Tenerife, during the Halloween break, days after the position was filled in an effort to come to terms with the outcome of the saga. As an energetic cyclist with experience of marathon running, I should have known better. I pushed myself into and beyond the safety zone, the mad zone, where cold logic and caution were ignored. It is sufficient to record that I hit the wall, and the wall beyond that again. Preparations were minimal, water in short supply, but more important than all these I missed the brake that my regular cycling companion would have applied had he been present. The call that should have been made went unwhispered. The four-and-a-half-hour slow climb to high altitude was more than had been bargained for. All told, a bridge too far, as a subsequent medical highlighted a minor heart irregularity, A-fib, in cardiac terminology. I still have not forgotten the extremes of heat on the ascent and the chill factor on the sixty kilometres freewheel descent to base, as my fingers froze on the handlebars.

It was a severe shock to the system in more ways than one as repeated 'de–fib' corrections in hospital, pads to the chest, 'stand clear,' forced me to be at the receiving end of an ESB bill. Reality registered quickly; it was time to face facts as health considerations and quality of life, once taken for granted, suddenly assumed importance. Time out was called. The word moderation, foreign to my vocabulary, began to creep in. With normality restored, or what passed for normality, and problems rectified, months later I resumed work. I had no option but to take the tablets and obey the good doctor. The bell for the last lap was welcomed reluctantly. The whole episode had defined real friendships on a personal level, and parked permanently long-held dreams of tackling a mountain stage of the Tour de France, not to mention calling in on former pupils scattered world wide. The thought of early retirement with dignity and health soon became a priority, now that my life was back in focus again. The ghosts had vanished, and happiness returned once more. I had learned a lesson the hard way, and in telling it here as it happened, I hope somebody else may benefit in turn.

I wish to apologise and thank in turn the pupil, who initially posed the question of disappointment in my last class. I trust he will forgive me for not giving a truthful answer at the time. In many respects, he forced me into self-therapy and to come to terms with a guilty conscience, especially as it gave me the opportunity to write it out of my system. Lying, or being economical with the truth where pupils were concerned, never sat easy with me.

Solvitur scribendo – it is solved in writing – I now understand and recommend this method of coping with life's roller coaster ride. Dare to be yourself; write or work it out of your system. Disappointment and rejection, if fed by bitterness or anger, consume like a cancer from within. Life is still beautiful, if we only take time out to appreciate and enjoy it. That last hurrah class and the question posed can at last have a line drawn under it and not before its time either. Deo Gratias; now I can rest easy at night with a door to the past finally and firmly closed behind me.

LIFETIME CHOKERS

'They say you played for Kerry, Sir?' a voice piped up from the front row in class. An innocent enough question you might think but I had learned from experience over the years to presume nothing. 'In an All Ireland, Sir, is that true?' Taken aback at his directness I wondered if someone had primed him to put me on the spot? Defensive and private with my answers on a sporting past I was economical with the truth; I rarely lied, just tended to over or under state as the occasion demanded. If other teachers wished to be familiar and cross the invisible line in their discussions with pupils furnishing information and ammunition, giving hostages to fortune, then that was their choice. When this innocent 'cherub' put the question, my suspicions were aroused. Was he probing a hidden past or simply interested in confirming the half rumour that surfaced every now and then that I had been to the top of the Gaelic mountain? In spite of the phenomenal growth of Gaelic in the college area, no former pupil had yet achieved the ultimate prize and gained an All Ireland medal. Some came close, like Moses they looked into the Promised Land, but never entered it. In this context then, the question was more meaningful.

The fact that I had trained college and local football teams in earlier years togging myself out in my hard earned treasured Kerry colours possibly bolstered his curiosity. Giving credence to the rumour, had I not acquitted myself with some distinction in the annual Pupils v Teachers games as a goalkeeper in the nearby playing fields, a legitimate forum for settling old scores? Had I not specialised in training keepers in the Assembly Hall, insisting that they be blindfolded in order to sharpen reactions. All these activities added no doubt to the belief even then as now that only eccentrics opted to play in goals. Who then could blame me if I slipstreamed and gained street credibility as a new young teacher when confused with my illustrious older brother who had won medals with Kerry? While there was no confirmation of the rumour that was abroad about my accomplishments, neither at any stage in my career was there a denial.

'Da said you were a good goalie, Sir, agile and fearless and forever roaring and organising the defence.' The least my questioner, Seán, deserved was marks for persistence. By now he was like a dog with a bone. Ignoring the second part of his comment I puffed with pride and accepted the high compliment for the three seconds it took for him to kill with a smile. 'Were there embarrassing moments between the posts, Sir?' A question prompted no doubt by the incredible, even laughable faux pas by the goalie in the previous night's soccer international on T.V. The line of questioning was now too close for comfort. How much did this individual really know?

The topic now broached I had successfully consigned for over thirty years to the oblivion of my sub-conscious like a sunken mid-Atlantic submarine, in the vain hope that it might never explode or contaminate its surroundings. Momentarily startled, now composed, an inner voice whispered at first before shouting for attention; this voice had for years been successfully ignored and denied, but not on this occasion. 'Come clean; face up to it once and for all before you finish your teaching days; at least give them something besides dry History to remember you by. Bottling it won't make the problem go away. Confess and be done with it.' Courage renewed, with a deep intake of breath, my reply when it came addressed both of Seán's queries, that of playing in the long ago and an embarrassment that haunted me over a lifetime.

Flashback this story to 1962, weeks before the Cuban Missile crisis made the world shiver, when the Kerry hotline informed me at two days notice that I had been drafted in as a late sub-goalie for the Minor Final in Croke Park. A latecomer to Gaelic at sixteen I had proved competent, borderline B+ in terms of school exam grading, or in local parlance, useful in the gap. Terrified outfield initially as a scrawny weakling I was finally pushed back, if not demoted, into the goalkeeping position. To the surprise of many I soon made the position my own. With this late call up, a young man's ambition was about to be fulfilled, with insufficient time to allow anxiety or nerves to mount. It was only within the secure confines of the family circle that the full story was ever recalled and retold ad nauseam by adult brothers who taunted me like children. Repression, I believe, is what psychologists term a conscious attempt to suppress and forget. Now in my half dotage, un-shackled and free I find it difficult to separate fact from fiction in what now has become a party piece as with each telling the story gathers legs. That I believe is the prerogative of every storyteller.

Only an imaginative sports journalist could successfully capture the spirit of those brief few hours in September. Catapulted briefly onto a national stage, Warhol-like I enjoyed my short period of local adula-tion; excitement mingling with the Senior team, gods in their own right, in reserved train carriages and a Bray hotel, before finally facing into a packed Croke Park of 80,000 that would horrify a modern Safety Officer. Supporters like spiders scrambled aloft on the corrugated rooftop of the corner Nally Stand, gingerly picking their steps as others clambered the drainpipes twenty feet high to vantage points where they held on for dear life. Elsewhere, circus-like, figures balanced pre-cariously dotted and straddled the high perimeter walls lording over swaying crowds on Hill 16. The muscle-bound, sardine-packed Hill and Canal supporters dared not even entertain the word 'Toilet'. At no stage did claustrophobia once enter into their vocabulary.

There I was pitch-side on the stage of all stages, overjoyed, overawed, about to fulfil the dream of a lifetime. My senior sibling, on duty for the Senior Game, kept a distant if watchful eye out for his excited jun-ior about to enter the August arena. Without fear of contradiction I can boast that I was the best kitted-out panel member of the day as my fa-ther, ever a devotee of sartorial elegance, had insisted on an after-hours private fitting in the local bargain stores before the journey to Dublin. A willing participant, oblivious and unconcerned at the visible creases in my new playing gear; I was certainly dressed for the part. A long-standing family tradition of dress code was going to be maintained on that special occasion. It's pointless to attempt to convey the tension in the dressing room where kidneys over functioned in an overpowering atmosphere of Sloan's wintergreen embrocation, the magic rub, guar-anteed to loosen tensed muscles. Gladiators in the wings in the dimly lit tunnel, we awaited the call, prepared for battle. On cue, to the clatter of cogs, we floated out onto the sacred turf to the cheering sea of faces in the stands. The subs, eager to serve, as always waited impatiently in the new concrete low-slung dugouts. We lived in hope, rare moments to be savoured and possibly sweeten the cold days of future Winters.

Fast-forward the contest. The worried Kerry selectors midway through the second half, three points in arrears to a rampant Mayo team, were forced to ring the changes. The order rang out – McMahon, you're on! A Roy of the Rovers scenario, direct from the Dell comics of my youth. Had I not played this scene over and over in my pre-match imagination, a final throw of the dice in an effort to turn the tide of battle? I swelled with pride and confidence pitch side. As the hero Matt of old stated, the pride of the little village was at stake, but in my case now, The Kingdom. The barked order, a war cry – over the top, a frontal assault – long anticipated, was now a reality. The incumbent goalie, a versatile player, was transferring to midfield making my entry possible, even essential with the minutes counting down.

But wait, the scene move by move in slow motion has been freeze-framed. A heroic solo effort by a forward finally unlocked the opposition defence – a sideways pass – finished in the roof of the net. G-O-A-L!! Alleluias rang out. Excitable at the best of times, I had scarcely removed my tracksuit leggings before I too took off —- vertically! Darkness closed in, blood flowed, the concrete ceiling still intact had been christened in style. It is indeed doubtful if I was ever worthy enough to grace the occasion, but concussed, confused and confounded lying prostrate on the sideline I certainly was in no fit condition to play any further part in proceedings. Goodbye Honolulu! Dream shattered! Medal gone! A right bloody mess, ten stitches to the skull, the sole casualty of the day!

And what's more, I wasn't even missed. The Kerry victories of the day, along with my brother's fastest goal ever in a final some twenty minutes later, scarcely registered with me. The ridiculous to the sublime, for my family high in the crowded stands, in a brief fifteen-minute period. Do I hear you titter? If so, spare me, as the delete button in my brain has been stuck for years and refuses to obey instructions. Such is life; what could not be cured had to be endured. Years later in my father's novel 'Hero Town' published posthumously, he wrote of hero 'Arsey Darcy' in similar circumstances, red-carded for fighting during such a final occasion as this, disgraced before the nation, 'shitting on the course' and bringing disgrace down on all concerned. Try convincing me that he didn't have me in mind when he wrote that passage! To this day my own children doubt that those lost moments of glory ever took place. Few if any outside the family circle were aware of the incident, fewer still were informed of it. I made sure my secret remained confined, until now.

However, to confound the doubting Thomas's, all is not lost. I have recently presented my case to the Kerry football authorities requesting an official acknowledgement on headed paper testifying to the fact that on this day of days in my life, more than forty-five years ago, even if untold trouble was caused, I was present, willing if incapable of representing my native county.

The 'Choker in Croker' is what one wise wag entitled the whole episode, appropriate in its own way. Embarrassment and disappointment were indeed my middle names. For any giggling audience let it be known that within a short hour of my downfall all was forgotten and forgiven in the celebrations of victory. An appropriate lesson in itself for modern youth to take on board is that the wheel turns, for every downswing there is a corresponding upturn. The world continued to revolve on it axis as it inevitably must. Few knew or cared about my mishap and neither was I the centre of any universe. Life went on regardless. Hopefully the smiling cherub who broached the question and put me on the spot will understand my reluctance to clarify or discuss the issue over so many years. Clear off now and leave me with my nightmares please!

****

"Do you know what I'm going to tell you now?'
 "What?"
"Now that you are unburdening yourself you should tell them about the Kojak episode."
 "Didn't we agree never, ever to mention that matter?"

147

"Why not? Sure you have nothing to lose now."

"Except a reputation, or what's left of it. I'd be the laughing stock."

"Come on. Give them something to talk about."

"And let them mark me down as one of the crazy gang in providing further proof?"

"You might regret not doing so. It could be your last opportunity."

"Ah, to Hell's Gates you could be right. I'll take my chances."

If this sporting Mecca was the most embarrassing moment of my life a close second was soon to follow. It is courting disaster to suggest that nothing in life compares with standing and admiring one's first new car in the driveway. I stress new as opposed to the succession of clapped-out bangers that most young married couples used to suffer when interest rates were in excess of fifteen percent. Picture me Saturday after Saturday; gardening abandoned, lovingly washing and polishing the gleaming Escort Estate. Didn't the great man, Henry Ford, call his popular model the Baby Ford? This now was my baby. Beaming with pride I catered for its every need. After one such weekend wash, the deafening loud clang of metal on metal jolted me from my kitchen table. Dumbfounded, my prize possession had inexplicably vanished, at least temporarily, now shunted some forty yards further down the road from its parked position like a wagon down train tracks. With a sickening feeling in the pit of my stomach I imagined all types of scenarios, robbery, hijacking etc. Worse for wear, with her rear-end concertinaed, the empty street held no explanation, only the receding tail lights of a speeding yellow car rounding a corner, was in view. Acting hastily, nothing new in itself, I set off in hot pursuit thankful that the engine at least turned over. Enraged at a shattered dream, hunting in sight and scenting blood I refused to let my world collapse.

Fight or flight, no dilemma presented itself, I intended to do both as the shoeless foot was pressed to the board. The crossroads further down posed no problem either as the chance appearance of a pupil answered my cryptic shouted query. "Yellow car, right or left?" I followed as instructed just in time to see the Sports Triumph merging onto the main road. As a fan of TV movies, had I not viewed even dreamed myself into such car chases in Frisco week after week? Where there was any deficiency in my imagination 'The Italian Job' suggested plenty of options and advice on possible courses of action. This was reality TV twenty-five years before its time. Kojak style,' Who Loves You Baby', lacking only the lollipop I hurled the car forward, came abreast of my target, swerved suddenly forcing and bringing the startled driver to a grinding halt on the pavement. A jumped exit resulted in a citizen's arrest, my first and last. The bespectacled, by now speechless diminutive driver gasped in disbelief, as did the onlookers in the nearby bus queue, all nameless extras in an afternoon drama. The immaculate, pristine condition of the grounded Triumph told its own story before it slowly dawned on me, as no doubt it will for some readers, that a terrible error had transpired. The Gardaí, quick on the scene, were of the same opinion. Embarrassment flooded in and overwhelmed me from all sides. Calculate the odds of two yellow cars exiting from my isolated road at the very same time especially when this colour next to snot-green was the most unpopular at the time in Dublin. Suitably assured and placated, blood pressure soaring, I finally released the vice grip on the coat of my fuming ashen-faced prisoner. I was under the mistaken assumption that the laying on of hands was an essential part of any arrest! A little knowledge particularly of the law is indeed a dangerous thing. On advice I withdrew from the scene allowing cooler heads to prevail, before quickly seeking refuge and solace in the adjacent Mill House pub. I needed no second invitation. To this day I believe the lawman was a parent of one of the pupils, as he seemed to know me!

In a secreted snug within, a black coffee, no not a pint, went some way in bringing me back to reality. The strong brew fortified and steadied nerves before facing and accounting for the sudden rush of blood to a distraught wife on the home front. Overall a disastrous faux pas, an embarrassment that to this day brings me out in a cold sweat. Where errors were concerned I had hit the jackpot. No half measures here; it was accomplished in style. Visibly shaken, I contemplated the possible legal consequences that might ensue. Shoeless still, I now knew that I didn't have a leg to stand on in any court of law. Hours later another stranger's timid knock on my door revealed all and admitted liability, which resulted in an agreed private solution to the whole problem. Who was I after all to contemplate pressing charges in view of events earlier in the day? To be forgiven, do we not first have to forgive? I never did obtain the name of the shell-shocked offended party I accosted. In all, a bad experience but an important lesson learned for life.

Thankfully our paths crossed again. Years later a house relocation and new parish resurrected the whole story as a troubled conscience refused to forget. On the Mass altar at the lectern, the readings were delivered, enunciated, acted and interpreted by none other than the offended and falsely accused driver. His startled terrified face had continued to surface in my dreams, there was no mistake on seeing him once more. As the months passed I failed to bring myself to approach and apologise, such was the weight of my shame. From a distance I admired this pillar of the church community, reader and altar server to an aged pastor. Finally emboldened I approached, reintroduced myself and confessed to this saintly man. On the church steps, as the winter solstice sun shafted a golden Newgrange beam through the open door and up the aisle to the glinting tabernacle, I begged forgiveness for past foolishness. He made it easy; few words were spoken. His nodding head and forgiving smile reflected the glory within that same church. Cleansed and forgiven by a fellow-Christian, inwardly I now glowed. The timing was fortunate as shortly afterwards with sadness I prayed for the happy repose of his gentle soul. He was indeed the silver lining to a very dark cloud that lingered far too long in my life.

What lesson did I take from this most shameful, awkward moment? It forced me to realise that inanimate objects like my beloved car did not deserve the attention lavished on them by foolish owners. Any surplus energy I had from that day out was now reserved for pupils wherever I encountered them, conscious too that others had yet to be converted on the Damascus road, as I was on that fateful day. There are sufficient embarrassing moments in this telling, to fill any person's lifetime. If there are others who harbour concealed moments of embarrassment that grow and weigh one down I strongly recommend confession, public or private, to oust those demons lest they be overwhelmed as I was.

Belatedly I have acquired the confidence to reveal all on paper - but alas I bemoan the lost opportunity of a live class telling as the printed word lacks real emotion and atmosphere. Embarrassing moments like memory can be capricious rather than pragmatic. We rarely choose what to remember, it chooses us.

THE KNOCK AT
THE DOOR

For wonderful and vague reasons, known only to themselves, former pupils now grown men with responsibilities found time when passing the school to knock on a classroom door, and call in on their former teacher and one time tormentor.

Did they do so to confront and exorcise demons and finally admit to themselves that the cardboard giants that dominated their school days were only human too? Were they pleasantly relieved now that time had mellowed memories, and greyed those self same spectres? Was the visit a one-upmanship gesture of defiance, that gave the lie to the dire warnings issued in the past, proof positive that not only had they prospered but matured in the new Ireland? Did they now view me as a latter day Don Quixote still tilting at windmills? If they did they were perfectly entitled to do so, as on numerous occasions I asked myself the same question when spirits were low.

As citizens of the world these men had many interesting stories and adventures which they were only too willing to relate and share there and then with me and the captive, delightedly distracted pupils. Only now do I fully understand the graffitied pupils' slogan on the art wall of the staff room, "anything for a free class". I marvelled at the achievements of these casual callers who visited, secretly surging with pride in spite of earlier fears and concerns, which were now allayed. Many were justified no doubt in retaining grudges and gripes even if they did not express them openly. They had indeed proved themselves in life routing any nagging doubts, which reassured me that I was not wasting my time after all, confined as I was over a lifetime within the four walls of a classroom. As a man among children divorced from the adult and pressurised real world, such confirmation was needed and always welcomed as I often chided myself that as a teacher one was at best a finger post – pointing out the road to Babylon, Cork, or San Francisco to adventurous young men about to leave my care, all eager and "mad" for the road. Many of these same roads I knew I would never travel myself. It was difficult not to be envious of their youth and success. Contented in the classroom; there would be no regrets. If they were welcomed back, it was because I wanted to see the finished product.

On the long school corridors they admitted to having little difficulty in finding me as more often they heard me before ever seeing me, finally screwing up the courage to knock and re-enter classrooms. As of old, they found me in full flight, teaching and pacing in the confined space like a caged lion. These are their words, and not mine I hasten to add. The age profiles that peered in the slit glass panel on the classroom door before entry bore only vague likenesses to those innocent youths of former days. The unexpectedness and unpredictability of such visits certainly broke the monotony of the school timetable. They were welcomed back as fledged family members, long gone now flying free in the great wide world outside. I never considered such visits an intrusion, unstructured, informal and welcomed as they were. Hesitant, yet confident, their first reaction on entry was to take in with a glance and nod approvingly at the blackboard scrawl where the time-worn diagrams and cartoons were recycled as if new. I could read their minds: "same old ding dong – nothing changes." Some no doubt, transported back in time, looked fondly in the direction of desks, many long since replaced that framed their early development. It was very often the business card gilded and embossed, trumped on the table with justifiable pride that saved embarrassment and blushes as I struggled to dredge up from the past a name to match the face. Nicknames and incidents – filed away and half forgotten clogged the information highway, and neither were they always complimentary.

When I mismatched and was confused they were understanding and forgiving, as I stood corrected, and grateful that the excuses I made were readily accepted. Had I not taught over 150 Byrnes and O'Briens, not to mention O'Connors, Sullivans and Ryans? It had come to the stage where even my own surname had lost all ring of familiarity as often I found myself shouting and chastising namesakes, forgetting that I was badmouthing a possible kinsman. For me it was always the individual and personality behind the name that imprinted itself – rarely the name. I had wearied pupils with half apologies on this score year after year, yet confounded many twenty years later when I reminded them of incidents and stunts pulled off, that many had wished forgotten. Surprisingly, voices and handwriting were rarely forgotten, but those with beards and moustaches always left me floundering to the extent that I doubted if I would have recognised my own son had he entered with such appendages.

Each former pupil, be he in his 30's or 40's, knew best why he revisited such classrooms. Did it satisfy a need to tie up loose ends and come to terms with the past, just like the urge that strikes to compile the family tree later in life? Had I not also looked in on my old teachers as an adult? Whether it was a coming of age ritual or closure on my part I never fully knew but I never regretted doing so. Now with the tables reversed I found it a rewarding experience if only because it filled in the bigger picture, stuck as I was with an image frozen in time, forever a teenager.

*****

'A healthy mind in a healthy body', the Latin phrase "Mens sana in corpore sano", has long lingered with me from my own school days. I subscribed to the ideal, put it into practice as best I could without achieving it, before inflicting it on pupils hoping that in time they might even half thank me for doing so. How easy it is to subscribe to lofty thoughts like this, when one can only dream of ever realising or witnessing it in the flesh. On the one occasion when the knock came and the young man entered, crossed the floor and placed the sagging nondescript shopping bag on the class table, I fully understood the true meaning of what I preached.

I greeted him as any visitor deserved. 'What's this?" I said. 'Open it,' he replied in a shy low whisper, obscuring the bag all the time from general view with his back to the amused pupils. The now revealed contents glistened. As quickly as I opened it he closed it again but not before reading the engraved inscription. ' New York Marathon winner, under 23 category.' 'I never doubted you,' I said adding with increased curiosity, 'I hope you bettered the three hour mark.' 'Two hours 32 minutes,' he admitted reluctantly.' 'Wow,' I gasped, at a time that might have seen him on a Olympic podium twenty years previously. At that point he discreetly withdrew the bag, closing it quickly.

Words such as perfection and Renaissance man flooded my brain. The trophy was proof positive indeed that one enlightened pupil at least had proved the quoted phrase was a possibility. His achievement in the race was just the final part of a long, long apprenticeship served in pursuit of the desired balance of mind and body. What Alex achieved and what I had witnessed over a ten-year period was as close to the ideal as I dared imagine. For years I had watched from a distance his progress within the school. On the academic ladder he was a late developer, surmounting reading difficulties only at a late stage. But when the booster rockets fired he took off and launched himself into trajectories that had to be revised and upgraded every six months. Academic barriers were smashed over and over again as if he was making up for lost time. Moreover he possessed a wisdom about life that I could only acknowledge yet never fully understand, an intelligence beyond academia, an enlightened clarity that came from a deeper level, a philosophy of living, an approach at such a young age that confounded and amazed me. I am slow to use the word genius but every teacher is I believe entitled to contemplate its usage once in life.

What was the spring from which he drank and drew sustenance? I can only guess and mention in passing that it was in the woodwork department that we first glimpsed his talent. Having spent a lifetime in service to two craftsmen I was quickly abandoned by my mentors as a lost cause when they saw the excellence of Alex's completed projects. They recognised perfection, and knew the gene pool stretched far back. His mother confirmed as much later in admitting that his grandfather had built the Queen's Ceremonial Coach in years past. We stood back, admired, directed and facilitated his gifted hands and talent to develop. We dared not intervene.

I believe I got a clue to understanding Alex, however briefly, when he privately admitted to me that meditation was part of his daily routine from an early age. Whether this was Transcendental Meditation, popular at the time, I never queried, as it was all foreign to me. Was this what gave Alex his centre, focus and understanding? Did this facilitate the fusion of mind and body, the dovetailing of energies that achieved the balance, which he redirected into the various levels of his life and activities? He had a philosophy of living, a natural awareness that found the middle way and expressed itself in whatever task he undertook. Time and time again I saw him surmount obstacles others would have turned their backs on. It is sufficient to instance the German he taught himself in eight months to qualify for University entry, as he was never afforded the opportunity to study modern languages in the classes he started out in. Nothing surprised me anymore. Perhaps it was the unity stressed in Eastern philosophy as opposed to the Western emphasises on logic and reason that took him to this level. I dip my toe and retreat instantly from waters that are far too deep for me.

The concept of a balanced and all round developed personality was no longer a slogan to be chanted about now that the reality existed before my eyes. If I continued to preach my gospel with renewed vigour when he left us for university am I to be blamed? Echoing the lines of the hymn 'Mine eyes hath seen the Glory', for the one and only time in my career, I had witnessed the incarnation of the ideal; he existed on a plane I only dreamed about. What a joy and pleasure it was to behold! More is the pity that I had not met him earlier in my own life and taken a few pages out of his book or accompanied him in his long march across the Pennine Chain. It would certainly have made me more reflective and less impulsive in my own struggle with life.

I knew little of his later accomplishments till the day he knocked on that classroom door. It spoke volumes for the character of the individual that he did not trumpet this victory locally. The normally perceptive school grapevine had failed to pick up on this Renaissance man. He saw to it that no one outside the family circle was made aware of it. In calling to the school he was crossing a personal Rubicon. Why had he visited? I interpreted his gesture as a simple sincere thank you for those of us in the school and 'Café' who had guided and assisted him years previously. My role, and it was a small one, was to introduce him to running, which he took to, training himself privately and turning out in big competitions when required. In sport as in life, he always set his own private targets.

I was not surprised when I heard that on graduation from university he went to work in Japan. I like to think that he was going home to an etiquette, culture and Zen philosophy that beckoned him east. This return visit was more meaningful to me than words can ever convey. I refrained from praising him, as his shyness and modesty were laudable if difficult to fathom. I was as proud at that moment as if it was I who had won the gleaming trophy. On leaving we smiled at each other, knowing looks that conveyed all, while the on-looking pupils observed without ever fully comprehending.

So perfection does exist after all. I persisted singing the same old song, the only one I knew, down to my last days in teaching. Achieve the balance and aim for the stars. Alex, while I never saw the lightning strike twice, wherever in the world you live I salute and thank you for allowing me to glimpse and understand more fully the perfection and balance I preached. Whoever said you can't teach an old teacher?

******

Occasionally in the classroom when the energy levels were low, I would stand and stare out the window at the framed Three Rock Mountain in its various shades of seasonal colours wondering what became of certain pupils whose names and faces surfaced like air bubbles from the pool of memory. One specific individual haunted me as I looked out directly on his village that nestled at the mountain base. To satisfy a nagging curiosity, on a dark winter's evening I ventured out hell-bent on finding out what became of him. Previous enquiries by his equally mystified former classmates had drawn a blank. Like an unwelcome politician canvassing, I knocked on doors. In the semi-rural community family surnames were still recalled and within the hour I had located his home. This was no ordinary individual; to me he was special. No other pupil had been elevated to the high pedestal that I placed him on. The Adonis-like image of my lost sporting hero imprinted on my memory only enriched itself with time. He was the benchmark that all others were compared to. Some came close but in reality he went unchallenged. Was what I saw in him the essence of that which the Greeks attempted to depict in their statues of marble? I had successfully convinced myself on this point.

In my native county where football was a religion, I had seen and met Mick O'Connell who had been almost elevated to the status of a living God. In turn I witnessed Ring hurl for Cork and cheered on Mohammed Ali when he boxed in Croke Park, making bold and seeking his autograph on the only scrap of paper I had on my person, Mao's Little Red Book, a document that dates me and which I still treasure. All these heroes of mine were flesh and blood, not just grainy TV images or dancing shadows on a cave wall, which many settle for today. Little then did I think that shortly after my transfer to Dublin I would be afforded the opportunity of teaching and coaching a youth who out-rivalled all other pupils with his ability and raw talent in the field games he played. I counted my blessings as any coach would in similar circumstances. Sadly due to the economic circumstances of the time he emigrated at an early age. Like a meteor he flashed across the night sky, yet in those few years I had seen enough to bolster beliefs that never changed. Our loss was another's gain I consoled myself, and bid him a fond farewell. His classmates' impressions, even today, echo mine as they too hold him in high esteem, even awe.

My quest on that winter's night twenty years later was a futile one, even alarming. His family informed me that he had gone to ground years previously, and was untraceable. If privacy was his desire, then his wishes had to be respected. My questions went unanswered but at no stage did I stop wondering and worrying about my lost sporting hero.

The occasion of the Charlton era in Irish soccer in the 90's was indeed a memorable time for many, and no less for me when the knock on the class door finally re-united us again. I welcomed him back; he was en route to Italy. Most teachers will admit that there is always one 'white-headed boy' over a lifetime who successfully breaches the outer ramparts of their reserve and privacy. Where fishermen talk of the one that got away, teachers talk of the lost talent. In his absence his status grew. Never did he realise the impression he had made on his former teacher and sports fanatic.

Now, he stood before me, after all this time, in appearance a totally different person, taller and older, a youth grown to manhood. To my shame I scarcely recognised him as he re-introduced himself shyly. I was as baffled as he was disappointed. It was his voice that rang a bell and saved any real embarrassment. Overwhelmed and overjoyed I believe I threw my arms around him in Spanish style oblivious of the pupils, who looked on amused at this private emotional reunion. Let me remind the reader that it is no easy task to project a frozen youthful image twenty-five years into the future and readily recognise it again. When I composed myself I introduced him as the legendary sportsman they had heard me wax eloquent about so often. Now it was his turn to be embarrassed as we applauded him loudly, having once again exaggerated his talents shamelessly.

It is enough to say that Tom and I are now in regular contact through e-mail and Skype. He has prospered in the business world beyond my wildest dreams. And still the personality remains unaltered by time. When I chided him for being out of shape and needing to shed a few pounds he accepted the censure commenting, certain teachers never change. On the occasion of his marriage in Australia I wrote a testimonial for his Chinese wife vouching that his clan held sway in Wicklow for the last one thousand years. To paraphrase the poet, 'he was of no mean people.' Recently his children who vaguely know me as a distant Irish voice, an old teacher, came across the penned words in a drawer and demanded that it be framed and displayed in a place of honour in their home. Now they are doubly proud of their father. Talent will out, it cannot be denied.

As a pensioner and reluctant traveller, if I ever pluck up the courage and energy to venture abroad, my first port of call will be Australia to accept the kind invitation extended. My questions have been answered. My concerns allayed.

Is it any wonder then why I always kept an ear cocked for a knock on the classroom door? I never knew what interesting person and story might walk in to enliven not only my day but also that of the grateful pupils. Those I have introduced you to represent many others who came back, a credit to themselves and a joy to have known. All were welcomed but little did they realise that I had learned more from them than they ever learned from me. Numerous others are also deserving of inclusion in my roll call, but where to draw the line? I trust that the personalities introduced on these pages will not be too upset on reading my tributes to them. That is if they recognise themselves in the golden light of a fast-fading memory that finds difficulty in separating fact from fiction.

******

And yet in retirement there still is no escape. The knocking still registers virtually if not in speech. A recent e-mail from a one-time pupil in Florida, now that I have finally gone online, reminded me that once in class I uttered dire prognostications on his behalf, out of frustration at his inability to shake himself out of his lazy habits. Years later he now informs me that those same words had haunted him for twenty long years like an accusing finger before finally impacting. Finally, he had marshalled his troops, assaulted the citadel and wished to inform me of a pending Masters Degree conferring, and a decision to take up a teaching post. It was a heart-warming and reassuring, if reprimanding text, which I appreciated. Important information in one way, but also a marker telling me in no uncertain terms 'get off my bloody case!' It was his way of silencing the accusing voice that he had lived with for so long. His wife, he added further, reported that he was now a different man to live with. I trust that in time he will in turn be active on somebody else's case.

Thankfully I still have my hearing and am ever listening with an ear half-cocked for a knock on my front door that might yet come. If it registers, it will be welcomed warmly, as all others were before it.

A RULE BROKEN

School and work; home and play, were always two distinct and separate worlds. I rarely if ever allowed one impinge on the other. In a small rural town such a separation is almost impossible to achieve, in the anonymity of city suburbia, miles from the school, the dividing line between work and home was easy to maintain. Looking back, I never knew which location was more desirable or beneficial as a teacher, the country town or the city, but if pushed I would have to opt for the community spirit of the small rural town where people lived in each others pockets, belying the squinting windows mentality which rarely, if ever registered with me – if it existed at all. In time the housing demands of a growing family in Dublin necessitated a move away from the Stillorgan school's catchment area that I loved, to the far-flung fringes of Foxrock where roots remained shallow. Thankfully it was closer to the sea that I could never live out of sight of, a throwback certainly to the Ballybunion seaside of my childhood.

At the end of each teaching day, I cycled home confident that I was able to leave the discipline problems and concerns for pupils behind me until the following morning. The bicycle wonderfully facilitated this mental turn-off as I distracted myself with anything and everything on the four-mile circuitous route home. In no way was I a creature of habit as I rarely followed the same road home twice having a dozen different houses in separate areas to call into for a chat - as the country man was wont to say, "When I'm out, I'm out." Gardens, home extensions, people waiting at bus stops, frustrated commuters in cars whose lives I imagined, even invented, all preoccupied me as the 'sediment of the day' settled in my brain. Workers at all level nowadays are strongly advised to respect the dividing line between home and work, but I doubt if the mobile phone has helped in any way to maintain this separation. It will come as no surprise to hear that I did not possess one and have no intention of acquiring one either. Not everybody has the luxury or ability to turn off when they cross the threshold; however I adhered strictly to the dictum that the two separate worlds would be maintained. On the home front, hedge cutting and heavy gardening were the physical outlets that counterbalanced any academic stress that surfaced in the working day. My class teaching, especially at senior level obviously necessitated preparation at home, but it was challenging, enjoyable and rarely gave me a moment's worry. If on the rare occasion in spite of best efforts, nagging concerns for pupils, which I always took seriously, surfaced at home it was only because I was seeking a missing jigsaw piece, the key that might unlock the personality of the individual in question. I never considered this aspect of teaching as work; it was simply problem solving at a human level, and where others had Sudoku and crosswords to entertain I too had my own games. The medical term 'stress' and whatever accompanied it was foreign to my vocabulary, and if such did exist camouflaged itself as ignored high blood pressure. I classified both as problems that visited themselves on older people, certainly not full-blooded young males with boundless enthusiasm and inexhaustible energy levels, such as myself.

How easy now it is to be wise after the passage of time. It was only when I found myself as a busy sports coach on recurring nights drifting in and out of unsettled sleep, selecting teams for upcoming matches, re-running old races or diving again and again as a long retired goalkeeper for the ever elusive ball that always evaded the outstretched finger tips, that I was finally forced to pay attention to the warnings and symptoms of stress. On more than one occasion on the school front I took myself in hand and withdrew from sports, which threatened on occasions to overwhelm me. I was a firm believer in the principle of 'Man know thyself,' even if it did take years for me to learn the lesson as all well intentioned advice from family and friends to conserve energy was politely ignored. These then were the boundaries I set myself on the home front where the topic of school and my involvement were never discussed with either my wife or four young children. I was a sustained self-sufficient unit, hell bent on doing it my own way, or not at all.

Naturally, as in many homes, the evening family mealtime conversation revolved around the children and their daily school experiences.

If it did, it took place out of my earshot. Reluctantly, as a coping strategy, I removed myself from this arena and dined American-style in front of the TV, in the adjacent open plan room within view and earshot of the family. How other teachers turned off from school, I certainly did not want to know about as this was mine and I was sticking to it. I am slow to recommend this anti-social decompression chamber stance unless one has the understanding and approval of a patient wife who monitors the all important table-talk highlights of a child's day. Today psychologists and parenting courses would condemn me out of hand for my actions. Any absence is partially explained and excused away by an obsession, a lifetime consuming interest in the six o'clock radio and TV news. I wallowed in the cascading headlines as an avowed junky. If the raised sound volume successfully drowned out the telling of many an interesting story by my children so much the better. It was only as adults that they admitted that they fully understood and finally forgave their absent and seemingly unconcerned father. I still admit to the occasional pang of guilt, on realising I missed out on an important phase of their lives. Consolation often followed when examination times came round; I made up for any lost time entering their lives again, monitoring, motivating, and providing assistance when required on those stressful occasions. As in any partnership my wife and I played to our strengths, fully appreciating that there was no apprenticeship served in raising children. In this manner I succeeded in distancing the school from the privacy of my home over all my years teaching. That is, with the exception of one memorable occasion when I allowed the defensive wall to be breached through my own inability to ignore and walk away from the flashing distress signals observed one early February morning in the school car park before classes had started.

The pre- Leaving Certificate mock exams loomed large on the morning I dismounted the bicycle, hands numbed on the handlebars from the skinning east wind. Any thing was preferable to fuming impatiently in log-jammed car traffic. Colder still was the piercing icicle look exchanged between a son and father when the door of the car banged as it pulled out of the school driveway. Nothing that had not been observed before, but when I over heard the throwaway comment and observed the shaking head of a distraught father who had once more chaperoned his only son for morning classes I sat up and took notice. The fault lines were there to be seen; the seismic tremor could not be ignored. Somewhat hastily I decided to follow my instincts. I often cursed myself for having a nose for trouble brewing in a tense atmosphere, long before any whiff of smoke surfaced, a trait that can be traced back to my own childhood. I have no doubt that many of the car-bound parents who passed and acknowledged me en route to school on my bicycle, deep down envied my freedom from rush hour chaos. Like Myles na gCopaleen's policeman, half-man-half-bicycle, my choice of transport kept me in constant touch and available to parents who casually but intentionally passed on information, concerns and phone numbers in our brief chance morning encounters in the school car park. Many informal appointments were made and kept in the few minutes it took to drop off a student for class; a direct line that always circumvented the best efforts of the school secretary's appointments book. I never underestimated those early morning encounters and observations since the daily masks had yet to be donned, faces were easily read and emotions often raw. On this particular morning the momentary cutting side-eyed glance from the shuffling agitated seventeen-year-old at his fuming frustrated father, flagged a tense relationship. The rifle shot of the banging door registered, loud and clear. A time bomb was ticking, had I not heard a silent scream for help? I could ill afford to ignore it as the pupil was well known to me; independent and gregarious, he was his own man and did not suffer fools or meddling teachers lightly. Well-intentioned Samaritans have their place, but father and son relationships can be like civil wars, best avoided by neutrals. I can almost hear the reaction of a reader, as he whispers, possibly even shouts, "Mind your own bloody business! Stick to the teaching you're paid for. Walk away." Sound advice in itself, but not for me on that morning. Rules were there to be broken, risks to be taken. This was one such occasion.

Later in the day when I casually met the student on the crowded corridor, I had my worst fears confirmed. There was no preamble. He bluntly admitted that he had his bags packed and was about to leave home. The pressure had got to him; he could tolerate it no longer. War had been declared and there was no going back. How often in class had I half-jokingly informed senior students, young adolescents, that something was very wrong if at some stage they did not consider their parents, particularly fathers, as old fogies, out of touch with the teenage realities of the modern world? This was a plea, as a parent myself, for patience and understanding for those of a different generation. The generation gap, parent gap, call it what you will, had to be admitted and accepted as a fact of life. How could we as elders expect to fully understand the adolescent's desire for freedom and all that was involved in the modern flux of morals, drink, drugs and sex; we who never had the luxury of contemplating such freedom, not to mention money in the pocket to facilitate such matters at a tender age. Were we now to be blamed as conservative parents in our attempt to hold the line in an age of rapid change, where the expression, "I want," "Now," "Me," and "I'm bored," challenged old values and shook our very foundations? This then was the gospel preached in class; an attitude and approach I honestly hoped might moderate and soften youthful impatience and restlessness with their out-of-touch seniors.

Intentionally I over-stated and over simplified the message with laughter and flippant comments in an attempt to get my point across, warning all concerned that within twenty-five years they might in time have a less jaundiced eye when similar responsibilities as future parents were thrust upon them. If nothing else, history I told them was littered with examples of yesterday's hot heads turning into tomorrow's conservatives. Young Turks will age and grow beards like every body else. More often than not my appeals and advice fell on deaf ears, but occasionally a scattered seed lay dormant for years before germinating, or so past pupils had privately confessed to in later life. Within hours the break-time crowded corridor, provided the opportunity to query the agitated scholar. If he had rage in his eyes he also had questions that disarmed me, as I had no solutions to the problems that he was grappling with. Sympathy and understanding fell far short of what was required.

I never worked out whether it was innocence, naivety or confidence that possessed me to offer my services as a possible mediator in a lifetime crisis for both father and son. A compromise and reconciliation certainly did not seem possible at this late stage. With communication bridges down, final year examinations and university prospects were suddenly seriously threatened. I felt my direct approach was justified on the grounds that desperate situations called for radical efforts. Inaction for me was no option because his voice would have haunted into old age. Better to try and fail than be a silent witness. Were I in his, or his father's shoes, I too would have clutched at any straw in the wind.

A hurried lunchtime phone call set up a meeting that same evening between the warring parties, in, above all places, my home. This proposal broke all my own ground rules, but I knew that the student trusted me as over the previous four years we had built up a strong relationship, since I had bailed him out on more than one occasion over minor issues. I was now entitled to draw on my credit, I believed. The parent needed no second invitation either; what parent would in similar circumstances? Gut instinct convinced me to act in haste. I had no expertise in conflict resolution or counselling; there again, were they required? If every willing hand or Good Samaritan required formal qualifications would any help ever be proffered? Were positions reversed I would not have spurned the good offices of another. The consequences of failure for all parties did not bear thinking about it. This, more than anything else concentrated minds, and elicited co-operation all round.

The meetings duly took place that evening. I stress meetings, much to the surprise of my family who witnessed me clearing and commandeering the 'good' room instead of tuning in and zonking out in front of the TV. Visitors, I hastily explained. "More Yanks," my son voiced excitedly. "I hope they are as interesting as the last couple," referring to a bizarre invitation issued by their unpredictable father the previous week following a chance meeting in the Montrose Hotel with an elderly Iowan tourist couple, total strangers, to come and visit a typical Irish family. Now, somewhat disappointed and grumbling, my son relocated his elaborate Star Wars station from the couch to the war zone under the stairs.

In due course the pupil duly presented himself at my door at seven sharp in the evening a full hour before his father was scheduled to arrive. Sheepishly he stood there wondering if the visit was such a good idea. The conversation that followed, or was it confession, after some soul searching and probing questions, that and a large dose of honesty, finally highlighted the nub of the problem and the reason for the extreme anger. Was it the neutral ground and a listening ear that loosened his bottled emotions? Spades were called spades. Progress was reported. Like a horse tangler at the fairs of old, bargaining positions were examined before minimum demands were quickly outlined on paper. I tried at times to nudge him in certain directions, but to no avail. He knew his own independent mind and bluntly expressed himself accordingly. The gravity of the situation was not lost on me. Terms agreed, I dismissed him after an hour out the side entrance to the nearby park for a walk, but not before depositing his list of five demands on the table to await the imminent arrival of his father. Points of concession call them, bargaining chips or ploys, which gave room for manoeuvre, were also amended.

The meeting that followed with his father was equally honest. He too was forthcoming, even when presented with his son's five points of demand. Naturally he had his own major areas of concern, and in his desire for reconciliation he in turn outlined five counter points which if conceded would provide a working basis for a family resolution and hopefully, peace.

 It was cheeky if not daring on my part to act as go-between, yet the compromise that resulted from the eventual face-to-face meeting between father and son showed a maturity that was a credit to both parties. The final agreed document, which I called The Ten Commandments, were formally witnessed and signed in my presence by the warring parties in that front room. When contracts were exchanged I discreetly withdrew and left father and son on their own for a short period. The frank and fruitful reconciliation was proof positive of the love and respect that existed within that family. Soon I was an impressed observer. I am not breeching confidentiality when I say that one of the points in question was as simple as a phone call home, like

E.T. in the film, to inform the anxious parent when a one a.m. post disco deadline could not be met. Easy access to working public telephones late at night back then, tested the patience of many parents who awaited the ringing tone and excuse as mobiles were yet an item of the future. When those long awaited phone calls were taken needless anxiety and final confrontation was usually avoided guaranteeing a nights' sleep for all concerned. Thankfully in this instance both parties finally emerged from the fog of confusion that threatened to overwhelm them. Contracts in hand, they came down from the mountain of hostility, fortified by good intentions. I opted out just as quickly as I had barged into the relationship. Bidding them a quick farewell, relieved and surprised, but not before politely suggesting to the father in a whisper that he could do worse than adjourn to the nearby pub, appropriately named the Magic Carpet, where as a goodwill gesture he might stand the prodigal son a pint.

This was the last I heard of the whole affair. The smile of contentment on the pupil's face in the following months in the run in to final examinations needed no explanation and was a reward in itself. The whole episode is now recalled with deep private satisfaction. Teachers, I further counsel myself, often delude themselves into believing and claiming false credit for outcomes to events that are well beyond their control. I knew better than to exaggerate the role played in the fleeting moments of a cold winter night. Any impact made may be as brief as a ten-minute time frame in which a sown seed may germinate. On this occasion I was no more than a person standing at a crossroads directing and facilitating a journey. It would not surprise me if the parties involved have long since forgotten the whole scenario. This is the reality of life and the nature of events; time, location and personalities are insignificant. The important factor was the end result and this is as it should always be. I was a fleeting facilitator, a bridge over which the parties crossed; no more, no less, the role played had limited significance.

Ever conscious of this fact over a lifetime in or out of class I refused to be offended when names and incidents got lost in the labyrinth that is the memory bank; in turn I expect the same degree of understanding from former pupils in this regard. The realisation that 'eaten bread is soon forgotten,' keeps a teacher's feet rooted in the reality of the moment, and I am mindful of the single past pupil who fell out with me, ten years after he left school, simply because I kept confusing his name with that of his elder brother. He took serious umbrage, worse still said so privately in a letter to me. Outraged, and in no uncertain terms I told him to take a running jump for himself.   In admitting to using the F...K word, I readily repent. After all I was expecting from him only that which I was more than willing to extend to him. Alas it was not forthcoming, both of us no doubt handled the situation badly and behaved like children in a playground squabble. The issue is mentioned in passing, as he was the sole individual I intentionally ever drew a line for and may have consciously wronged in the process. Homer nods too. No, not the Simpson one!

A brief act of kindness, it has to be understood, will be quickly forgotten; but the thank you in words, sincere and forthcoming as they were from father and son on leaving, with contracts signed, are still treasured and remembered. Similarly an injustice done, a wounding sarcasm, a promise not kept, a slur thrown, a prejudiced or racial attitude extended, will remain and fester in the subconscious of any offended pupil for life. This in time may be fruitful ground for anger and resentment that could scar and sour relationships for years to come. Mistakes and errors made in this regard always haunted me on the grounds that if offence was taken I was unlikely to know about it and certainly have little opportunity to make amends and apologise. Teachers must be conscious of this fact on a daily basis. Is this the millstone, the evil and cancer that the Bible railed against so strongly? Consequently it behoves all in positions of authority to register the fact and cogitate on it at regular intervals.

In inviting this little drama into my home, I realised I had broken my own rules about separating home from work. Might there be a repeat performance? In all honesty the answer is, that I would have to think seriously and twice. In the world we live in today one shudders to think what could have followed had a situation, fraught with danger, been exacerbated. Thankfully their maturity prevailed, but maturity cannot always be taken for granted. That cry for help in the early hours in the car park was heard and responded to, but what of the silent cries that go unheard and are often registered only in grim statistics? I had learned an important lesson that on occasions help must be offered despite risks to oneself. Never the less I intended to be more circumspect with any future offers of help. Advice, when forthcoming, was never given lightly, limitations and boundaries had to be recognised, but equally responsibilities to those who sought advice and support. Whether they asked for help or not I wished them to know that it was available from that day out on strict conditions.

Certainly in this front room confession, reason triumphed in a private family misunderstanding, but on the important issuing of bullying in school, in or out of the classroom, reason could not always be relied upon. This sensitive matter deserves serious attention though at times the media over-emphasise the issue. There is no doubt that bullying exists at all levels of society, but to what degree it manifests itself on the school front only a teacher's eye can know. Once or twice a year a parent would tell me in confidence that their son was the target of a bully. Once verified, if requested I moved in and brought the pupils together, innocently extracting both from classes on the pretext of needing assistance in the sorting of football gear or some other such excuse. Generally I called a spade a spade, outlined the evils of bullying and threatened that if it did not solve itself there and then, with apologies all round and a genuine hand shake, I would enter the equation and solve it by taking action, and failing that, go higher. My belief is that it is best to face down the bully squarely and deal with the issue on the spot, as invariably the bully will not go away. All I know is that this worked time after time and the problem rarely surfaced again. With such experiences the issue did not in my opinion live up to the billing it received in the media in general. That was my honest experience of the question over all the years. Today's youth are sensitive in the extreme, and the cut and thrust of the playground of old seems to be gone. Parents are more prone to read things into situations and words that were never intended in the first place. I fully realise that I was a dinosaur from another generation who thankfully never had to come to terms with the experience of mobile phone bullying etc., that became a practice after I retired. However, popularity in the playground and inclusion in matters cannot for any young individual be guaranteed or assured. Respect can be demanded and is deserved at all times as a basic right, but it also can be earned. I make these strong opinions in the full knowledge that a pupil who sat in front of me for two years, unknown to me was bullied, and felt it necessary to change schools to escape the torture. His parents brought it to the attention of the school, only when the transfer had taken place. I was gutted and blamed myself for not picking up on the matter.

If I never knew when a success was achieved I generally knew when a failure registered. It was proof positive that the road still to be travelled had corners and obstacles to be negotiated. To the very last day spent in harness I was aware that there were more lessons to learn than I ever had to teach.

REALITY CHECK

'Anything for a free class.' The artistic graffiti still screams in letters writ large on the corridor wall outside the school staff room. This special mural, the combined work of a talented sixth year art class, stood the test of time and was admired over the years, but not by all. The artwork, two by three metres, was chaotic, ageless in theme, Dali-like and nihilistic, and lighted up a featureless long stretch of fading yellow unplastered internal corridor wall. It's hard to imagine that this same wall was the topic of a heated discussion, as a proposal that it be painted over and obliterated was narrowly defeated at Union level - shades of a Cultural Revolution dictate or censorship from a darker past. Thankfully individuality, prized as it was in our august establishment won out over the conformity that some sought as a preferred option and safer bet. In disputes such as this I supported the underdog, rebellious youth, as a product of the flower-power psychedelic age dominated by the Beatles and Elvis. I chose to rely on my own compass and set course accordingly. Expect the unexpected, challenge the certainty, ride the random, all are perhaps better phrases to describe what took place in senior classes when I would occasionally announce, 'Books away gentlemen. Question time. Anything goes.' Needless to say the beaming faces and muted cheers of 'Yes,' together with the relaxed atmosphere that followed such announcements more than justified these 'pit-stops' on the educational road.

If only on stocktaking grounds I could justify myself to any forum of educationalists in sallying forth, classifying such forays as reality checks. I refused to confuse examination demands with education. Diversions about life recharged batteries, shunted staleness, rewarded good work and provided pupils with an ideal opportunity to question those who did not always profess to know the answers. Important questions raised could be aired in this informal forum and it was a very foolish teacher who did not listen; besides productivity always seemed to take giants steps when we reverted to the course work again. Many often too shy to ask openly did so privately on paper, when drawn from the suggestion list provided. The process was not as unstructured as it seems since I had various topics, outside of History, that I wished to tease out. Like the Dáil Question Time, I could conduct, lead and predict the course of topics for discussion and where omissions from my own set agenda were highlighted, I willingly yielded the floor to other issues raised. There was method in my madness.

Formality suspended, the line of questioning and topics raised were predictable, slow and tentative. The livelier pupils of which there was never any shortage availed of the freedom and initially led the charge. 'My father still talks about the day you caught him on the hop, Sir.' 'You are teaching here for ages. Do you never get bored watching the conveyor belt, bringing in young pupils year after year and then waving them off goodbye after Leaving Cert?' Trivial questions in themselves, essential sparring and warm-up for topics I knew would surface later. Over time issues current in society were echoed in these classes; violence, death, justice, relationships, values, friendships and racism in sufficient depth to give food for thought. The occasion gave pupils an opportunity to talk on important matters that might be teased out and aired, conscious that other teachers were similarly engaged in this process. I wished my teachers of old had done so. At no time do I recall being asked as a student in secondary school an opinion on any matter outside the course content. Who would believe me in admitting that I was too shy to ask, had the opportunity been given? As a student our train tracks ran straight and narrow with few junctions and no sidings. I saw to it that there would be no repetition of this policy.

Month after month I waited for the one topic that I knew the pupils would never raise. The topic of death was always overlooked, if not avoided, understandable considering their age; nevertheless I introduced it time and time again as it featured high on my list of priorities. I had ample opportunity to gently introduce this one topic, generally on foot of a pupil's relative who had sent in good wishes to his old mentor. 'Ah yes, I remember, young once, sitting in this very same class before he scampered off into life to grow old like you will in due course, leaving me behind again with extra memories. But not all grow old,' I would add, inching closer to the discussion I wished to generate.

'Some stay young forever; they are still here.' Puzzled, they demanded explanation. 'I speak of the ghosts, the spirits of those students whose faces I still see; they inhabit and haunt these very classrooms and shall be for me forever young. They never left. All died young, far too early. They still linger here, silent if often questioning. Call my ability to see them a sixth sense.'

The hushed silence in the classroom always indicated that my listeners were hooked. In this charged atmosphere I was off on the subject that never failed to halt and challenge them in their tracks. It was never introduced for entertainment purposes or shock therapy, as I was forever conscious of the sensitivities of my audience. They had their own family histories that I was not privy to, their sacred space had to be respected. The pallor of a few at the mere mention of death was sufficient proof that the well of emotion was close to the surface, sometimes even bubbling. For the majority it was an unknown territory, best avoided, that is if they ever thought about death in their young busy lives. This I believed was an omission that needed to be addressed. When the awkward question was raised it was in a positive manner focussing on the beauty and value of life, short as it might be, rather than on the finality of death. In some ways this challenged the invincibility and the invulnerability of modern youth. I like to think that I did so with humour, humility and respect. Avoiding the topic was too easy an option and one would have been neglectful in preparing pupils for the only ultimate stark reality in life.

In the close confines of those sixth year classrooms, in a dream-like fashion, they were informed that Barrett smiled up at me as ever from his window seat. I did not have to close my eyes; he was still present. The pupil occupying his onetime seat was often uncomfortable and self conscious Turning my head to the second last seat by the wall I shifted my gaze to a fair–haired Gavin, furiously writing away in a forlorn effort to complete his Irish essay within the allotted time. His copy lay uncorrected on my office table for two long years after his death, a sad reminder of the brief part that both of these special pupils were allowed to play in the game of life. As night followed day the impact of these words followed predictable lines, now that the audience were chilled into silence and deep thought. With the class unit duly shattered into individual shards, each was now isolated on his own bench that became an island. In this vein the roll call of names of the twenty or so former students whom I had once taught was taken; all permanently absent but not forgotten in the school, certainly not by me in the various locations that I associated them with. 'Nancy and Mary?' As láthair – absent, our liberated friends, no longer closeted, powdering their faces at the mirrors, as ever caring and kind and non-threatening in a less charitable and accepting era in the long ago. Like advance scouts they blazed a trail for those who were to follow and have their individuality enshrined in the laws of the land. There too was Bosco, the entertainer with Kerry connections; the fun-loving Malcolm in far off Thailand, and still standing tall Esso in his chosen corner at the window, while Brian skilled and brave forever hurls the ball, thump, thump, against the wall. A brief glance through the window would reveal quiet Craig ambling as ever so slowly through the school gate, dragging on a final smoke, reluctant to enter the school early, certainly not before the corridors were well aired. All in turn like sentries guard their carved out spaces, glancing occasionally at the door for the next reluctant entrant to enter and claim his place on the crowded list. The whistle blew for you also Larry, called to the line before fulltime as you walked the short walk from the nearby Highridge. As it did for Wynner who never fully filled his canvas with the bright colours he loved. All in turn were remembered by Father Seán in his library Mass, not long before he too joined them, leaving his African mission incomplete. 'Go ndéana Dia trócaire orthu go léir.' If they and many others are assembled now, in due course they await the arrival of an ageing teacher who would gladly give them one more class. I laugh at the prospect of lingering on these corridors in their company, but not just yet. Who knows, I might even possess a bicycle to chase down future generations of pupils yet to come. What better way might one be remembered than this?

Each name recalled, unknown for the greater part to those listening, registered momentarily. The arrows had struck home. The students, now withdrawn, digested and comprehended more fully. Sadly, death visited itself far too early on these young lives, leaving me in the school with fading images as constant silent companions while at home broken families silently grieved. The harsh finality of death was in every sense the flipside of the spinning coin of life. I resisted the temptation to overpaint the scene now conjured up. The pensive mood in the room vouched for hidden echoes in their own lives.

Sensationalism, insensitivity and fear had no role to play in any part of the discussions on death. On the contrary, to relieve any possible unease that may have crept in I regaled them with stories of my own initial contact with death as a youth in rural Ireland. I was attempting to take the inexperienced by the hand to the point where they might appreciate not only the gift and reality of life, but also its twin brother death. In the modern world this word has been devalued, avoided and sanitised and its impact is disguised in statistics. Mention any word you wish but avoid the word that pulls no punches. Dead- Muerto-Marbh. Be polite and substitute casualties, fatalities or M.I.A's. as in war. Whatever you do be sure to use the polite words - remains, in repose, removals and caskets - in ordinary conversation. Consign corpses, coffins, tombs, funerals and graves for horror movie reviews only. No great surprise then if today's children are distanced from the only certainty in life?

How could I convey to my class the reality of Paddy The Dead, our gravedigger long ago? No doubt he too had many a conversation similar to 'Alas poor Yorick, I knew him well.' How do I describe the character of Nell, the local Angel of Death, who when called, abandoned her kitchen chores to wash, shave and make decent the corpse for the house wake to follow before the final journey in Ned The Dead's hearse? Did I not as a youth personally test every coffin for size and comfort in Galvin's joinery yard and in mock imitation lie in state for my peers to view? Dare I tell them that as schoolboys we scoured the town for any door with a black crepe, indicating a death within, which always guaranteed at least a bottle of Nash's red lemonade and sweets if lucky, for the devout youthful mourner; a princely reward for any child with empty pockets in the dark 1950's. A return visit if made in the afternoon to touch the hand of the corpse as a final farewell, provided people witnessed the gesture, was equally rewarded and commented on favourably. Doubling up we it called it – scoring twice. Did we not as children keep tally on the horses and traps and later still on the number and models of cars that slowly trooped to the local grave-yard? Harmless entertainment, in which records were made and bro-ken in turn with advancing years. We as children certainly served our time as professional mourners. With the rubrics observed and mourn-ing masks discarded in the alleyways of the town we scoffed our good-ies and learned quickly never to over-play our hand as we monitored the overall health of the aged community, reckoning the quick-mouthed prayer for the departed soul a small price to pay. Ghoulish thoughts and fear were not in our vocabulary as entertainment, devil-ment and goodies took precedence.

Was I now, an adult and teacher in these school classes, attempting to explain the fundamentals of life, or merely trying to justify my own obsession with death held since childhood? Does this explain the im-pulse to visit cemeteries when abroad? If so allow me to strongly rec-ommend Genoa. Those enlightened certainly appreciated the funnier and lighter side of a telling which I believed was a positive and healthy approach to a much-avoided issue. Now that the dreaded 'D' word, mystique dispelled, had been introduced genuine open discussion often followed. With the exception of the few pupils who had lost a close relative, the relevancy of death for many had scarcely registered. On occasions when the line of questioning queried the spiritual and after-life dimension I felt like a cleric preaching from the pulpit.

Laughter for me was a more effective tool than all the dead bells ring-ing in the nearby church belfries nestled at the foot of the Dublin Mountains. It may have been an unusual approach but new ground was broken. The issue was at least brought to the forefront of their con-sciousness where I hoped it would remain as an accepted fact of life. If knowledge is a defensive mechanism, ignorance and denial will rarely sustain or prepare one for life. In this context Max Mitter's words deserve attention.

'It is curious how forgetful we are of death, how little we think that we are dying daily and what we call life is really death and death the be-ginning of a higher life.'

Now for the first time the memorial plaque to a former pupil, Mark, unnoticed by many in the bustle of school life, located on the exit gate of the school, assumed an added importance. Our young cyclist who, had he lived, would now be in his forties was killed instantly as he careered out of the gates into the path of the approaching minivan. Alas, he had no escape; death was brutal and quick. Time had not faded his memory. It may have been years ago but I can still see his young body sprawled as in sleep on the road, beside the mangled bicycle, as I too cycled out the same gate clutching in my hand an entry form for the Dublin Marathon at the height of the jogging craze in the eighties. Sadly, Mark had been cheated out of life while my insignificant race had yet to be run. Close encounters with death such as this are not easily forgotten. Many admitted that the story now personalised would remain with them for life. They, like me, often utter a silent prayer when passing out the same school gates. His desk in the First Year classroom two rows from the window, three seats back, was never empty for me, much to the consternation of the juniors who tenanted it year after year. Mark's lease was in truth a brief one, evicted at thirteen, the youngest of all in the cherished list of lost former pupils.

How do I begin to describe Barrett, for that was indeed his real name, a promising popular personality who smiled all through his silent suffering? His illness, Cystic Fibrosis, a condition unknown to me at the time, was an eye-opener as no doubt his story was for many an attentive hushed group. Battling monthly, in the hope of a transplant he refused to yield to the frightening statistics and the inevitable prospect of a young death. He clung to life and his portable oxygen unit, and bombarded daily with one hundred plus tablets a disease that counted down the clock. Over years, heroically supported by his family and close friends he faced down crisis after crisis. It was a humbling experience getting to know this humorous live wire both in school and at home during his long confined illness. When he travelled that lonely road he never did so alone. He was the essence of optimism and those in his circle learned lessons for life. The courage shown diminished yet enriched those who witnessed it.

While it raised profound questions that were well beyond my answering, it gave a new perspective on life and its value. He never knew the influence his struggle had on others around him. Life and death issues such as his, once personalised, could not be ignored. Words such as dignity, integrity, philosophy, life and its meaning, became linked to his name. Racked with infections and disappointments he battled on, but not before presenting himself, ever enthusiastic, in a tuxedo for an awards presentation at his Leaving Graduation Dance. Only the oxygen tripod prevented him from being hoisted like a triumphant hero on willing shoulders in the thronged function room as the waves on the nearby Killiney beach crashed in applause. Mawkish sentimentality never once entered the equation. Homage was paid to the genuine article. Months later, skin blistered all over in St. Vincent's Hospital, his brave battle came to an end. En route to Croke Park I had requested that my then sixteen-year-old son accompany me to Barrett's bedside for one last time with his parent's permission in the vague hope that my own too might witness the fine line that existed between life and death. Smiling as ever, the patient in the bed accepted and played the black cards dealt to him. His lesson was not lost on either of us, or on the various classes who admired his bravery. Who then can be surprised if I say that his presence was felt powerfully by me each time on passing his desk, a wall seat, looking out on the playground? For the flag you flew proud and high, Barrett, we remember and salute you.

On a related topic the stark suicide statistics, cold obscenities in themselves, scream from newspaper headlines. '456 dead, 11,500 admitted to hospital with 'self-inflicted wounds'. This shattering and inexplicable plague, accompanying the Celtic Tiger, visited on our younger generation is indeed a curse that defies comprehension by an older generation, which I represent. Will we as a society have to wait another fifteen years for the enlightened psychiatrists, educationalists and sociologists to forward theories that explain this new phenomenon? Must we suffer silently and stand guard as suicide stalks and snipes randomly those who find difficulty coping and communicating when depressed with the frustrations and expectations of life, before giving up all hope, they finally snap and exit the system? All this is sadly incomprehensible in an age of mass communication, technology and plenty.

These shocking and sensitive tragedies were rarely if ever discussed in the classroom during my teaching career. If this taboo topic of suicide ever surfaced at all, it did so in cold factual statistics. The subject, outside of the occasional short page in a textbook, was avoided and left untouched, in spite of the fact that many could put a story and a face to unfortunate victims in their own community. We, like many educational establishments were not left untouched by this horrific scourge. In truth, it was a blight that spread its malignant influence across the extended school family, and right into our classrooms, claiming victims as it went.

On such occasions, stunned, we spoke in hushed whispers. Authorities at all levels were reluctant to discuss openly, or offer any worthwhile advice even when the epidemic took on national proportions, which shamed and half-provoked them out of their laissez-faire attitude. There are many who would say that a response when forthcoming was tokenism at its worst. It is indeed a sad reflection on a society that leaves it to popular phone-in radio shows to air the subject openly. Wrong forum it may have been, but it was at least a wake-up call for society. No doubt experts agonised behind closed doors, highlighting stress, depression, addictions etc., as partial explanation, but if they did, very little solid advice percolated down to teachers like myself who often considered ourselves to be in the trenches. Never once can I recall being offered advice, courses, leaflets or even an in depth discussion on the question of suicide by any knowledgeable source. Behind all this approach, was the ever-present fear of the copycat theory that stifled and silenced teachers into, dare I say it, submission? One had to be a brave or foolish teacher to risk breaching this omerta. (Contrast this inaction with the present human Swine Flu scare.) I would have welcomed advice from any quarter, but it never came. Teachers who are considered front line troops in government campaigns for a variety of other problems, drugs, drink, sexual education and moral codes, were overlooked totally in this matter. The traditional approach in the past had been to get the message out to the younger generations via schools. 'Catch them while young,' but sadly this was not the case with suicide and depression.

Inadequate and helpless as we were as teachers, we observed from a distance and muddled on each in his own way. This was of little comfort or assurance to someone like myself who was responsible for some hundred and fifty teenagers. I lived in fear that something might happen on my watch and when it did the question of guilt or failure to pick up distress signals had to be lived with. Like an avenging angel, the dreaded visitation took place too often in the local and school community. Nothing ever prepares one for this sad and devastating news. There is no armour to shield behind, only inadequate coping strategies. In this context, the parachuting into our midst of so-called expert school counsellors, for a twenty-four or forty-eight hour period in the wake of such a school tragedy, while well intentioned and good P.R., sidelined as silent spectators the very teachers who were closest to the traumatised pupils. The pupils overnight were now expected to bond, however temporarily, with total strangers who would as quickly disappear out of their lives again within two days. It may have given the impression that the relevant authorities were in control and taking action; to me it was cosmetic, and undermined those very teachers who would still have to pick up the broken pieces when the 'visiting circus' departed. There has to be a better policy than this that can be implemented to offer hope and assistance for all concerned.

The 'if only' haunting and tormenting questions that lingered in families and schools after suicides are futile yet understandable attempts to put shattered lives together. In themselves they constitute a black hole that devours light and explanation. Some who suffer find solace in spiritual mantras, while others still sleepwalk through life, marking in their hearts significant dates in the yearly calendar of a lost life. The sooner help, advice or procedures can be put in place to simply understand this current plague and help reduce the incidence of suicides, the less the pain will be in the community overall. Time lost can never be regained. I hasten to add that little blame can be attached to any individual school or Principal who operates within the current confined framework. A solution or coping strategy, if it exists at all, must come from a much higher level, and yet if the budgetary allocation and promotional campaigns from central government sources for this the most serious malaise in our society over the last ten years are examined, they will be found seriously wanting, even shamed. The stark statistics today sadly and accusingly are registered higher than road fatalities. I need remind nobody of the monies spent and priority given to the road carnage question. What figures in suicide must be reached before the issue is properly addressed? In my own limited circle, in and out of school over the last twenty years sadly I name upwards of fifteen suicides and thankfully only a single road fatality. These figures speak for themselves. When will any worthwhile support or instruction be given to teachers who feel it necessary to scan daily the faces of those entrusted to their care? Must they continue to muddle on as best they can like I did, often in ignorance? Hopefully no reader will ever have to sit across the table from afflicted and distraught family members and attempt to explain why nothing registered on the radar screen, after another precious life has inexplicably ended. Perhaps this may explain to some of my past pupils the reason why my office door was always left open, in the off chance that a distressed pupil might take up the invitation and hopefully reach out. This simple gesture, I know for a fact, defused many a traumatic episode for pupils who struggled with darkness and despair. If there were other strategies that I could have adopted, I never knew about them and doubt if I would ever have been encouraged to adopt them.

It was always the bell that called time on my ramblings during these classes, which occasionally may have turned into monologues. Did the path chosen wander into pastures of Philosophy? Had Socrates not written, 'The philosopher is the man who should profess death, and learn how to die oneself'? Surely freedom is implied in the acceptance of death, or was I simply reflecting my own strong Christian beliefs? Does the fear of death reflect a fear of annihilation? If so the world war lessons of the twentieth century were lost on many. Certainly there was a therapeutic effect in raising the question of death in the first instance. In today's world we have no such taboos when talking incessantly about sexual matters, natality, even abortion to the new self-appointed gurus in phone-ins and the media in general. Is this the new pulpit of the twenty-first century? Morality and philosophy as themes are pushed further and further down the queue behind Big Brother and Ronaldo's soccer transfer fee.

If the pupils were at times bored with the issues raised, they were still tolerant and sufficiently interested to encourage me to continue with the policy. I was contented that they had now been exposed and informed on important issues. Thankfully nobody ever dared to object, since it was a small price to pay for a free class, which incidentally also exempted homework. This, after all, was a lesson for life, not just for one brief session. Invariably the class concluded with the lines I found scribbled in an old manuscript:

'We squander health, in search of wealth
We toil, and sweat and slave.
We squander wealth in search of health
And only find a grave
----- not by appointment!'

For the single worried pupil who admitted to me years later that a class talk on death changed his life utterly, I stand over the policy adopted in those 'free' classes.

THE CLASSROOM

If this was the memoir of a shopkeeper, by now in the reading you would have a fair knowledge of the customers that called in to the emporium. But what of the goods sold over the beech-grained counter over forty years? A limited stock, certainly, just History in all its shades and forms, which I twisted and turned, coloured and packaged, like candy rock until it became more appealing to the palate. Rarely was sight lost of the need for the balance, objectivity, and integrity that were absolute and essential requirements in any daily transaction. I was intent on imprinting History on sensitive young minds and if in the process other items like ambition, self-discipline and common civility were included, it was only what any generous grocer threw in regularly for good measure and luck. I make no apologies if slogans like 'Manners cost nothing and buy a lot,' etc., were packaged and recycled as words of wisdom and duly passed on as currency to another generation. The whole process and my personality were inseparable in the transaction.

In those early days the strict insistence, possible obsession that all textbooks and journals had to be covered, valued and respected together with the immaculately presented home work scrutinised daily, not forgetting the checking of the Carnegie Library membership cards week after week, no doubt labelled me as a bit of a crank. All were a throwback to my own youth where 'hand-me-down books' and a penny in the pocket were the order of the day. While never a big-time scholar I realised very quickly in the new setting that I had scholars to teach. My enthusiasm for History and teaching was as a result of having been taught in turn by an energetic and motivating nun in university who branded me for life. Slowly confidence grew and with regular feedback from senior students my teaching technique improved. Ever a firm believer in the need for self-assessment and critique, I never shunned the opportunity to improvise, and adapt well-established methods when the situation called for it. Since school and teacher assessment was a very late policy adopted by the Department of Education, I missed out on this essential feed-back which would have been welcomed, though the Unions initially feared and shied clear of such a policy. Compared to the sink or swim immersion in my initial posting, the Dublin challenge was less demanding, yet equally rewarding. Today's pupils have no concept of how boring and dry history textbooks of my secondary school days were. How anybody ploughed through dry factual statistics, and blow-by-blow accounts of wars and revolutions and still wound up studying the subject, leaves me mystified. Soulless personalities were but names on the page, without flesh or blood. It left a bitter taste in my mouth that lasted until the avalanche of the new modern textbooks, which thankfully swamped us in the years that followed. Many would agree that teachers today suffer from an overabundance of choice, as the May-time staff room range of complimentary textbooks will testify. Duly armed, I was in no doubt about the road to be taken in the teaching of History, which even in its spelling, has the word 'story' in it and as such I was going to tell it as an interesting story. Over time if students, influenced by this approach, agonised along with Luther as he struggled with his scruples, understood O'Connell as he galvanised a silent people and sympathised with Gladstone's obsession in securing a fair deal for Ireland, all the better. Where the Dublin folklore of Larkin was a fading memory they could do worse than stand beneath his imposing statue in the City centre and behold the passion of Big Jim raising hell and embracing Christlike the poor in his outstretched arms. The towering figures striding across the landscape of history never failed to interest and impress pupils. Hero or villain each deserved a proper hearing. Those who did not study History I believed missed out on life's drama.

For the younger minds the concept of time in History was a major stumbling block. The past, be it five, fifty or one hundred and fifty years, was all a distant fog. Yet the simple device that I copied and recommended to younger teachers in turn dispelled this. Put simply it brought up the image of a student positioned at the class blackboard stretching back his hand to his grandfather and extending the other hand in the opposite direction to an imagined future grandson. In that simple act the hands spanned a possible five generations, the equivalent of a minimum one hundred and fifty years. This simple imagined 'time machine' equipped the young mind to grasp the concept of time and allowed them to mentally jump, as it were in chunks, beyond Parnell, then O'Connell, Napoleon, The Boyne, Kinsale etc, in turn back along the centuries with ease. Imagine their surprise on the occasion of the Millennium when I introduced for interview a sprightly one-hundred-and-one-year-old lady, a family friend, whose grandfather could have fought in Waterloo. The point was not lost on them. She entertained them royally. I recall her standing and talking to the seventy plus pupils asking me in a loud voice the age of the group in question, to which I replied, fifteen years. Her reply and silent smile, which went over the heads of the pupils, was a throwback to the Victorian age in its utterance. "My goodness, but they are just on the point of the peppermint." If anyone blushed it was me. I know what she meant, yet no old person I subsequently asked, had heard this expression in reference to sexual possibilities all still in their future. Time in history, with such visitations and approaches, ceased to be a problem for many.

I wasn't always so clever as for years I failed to invite in the Overend Ladies; the Rolls Royce drivers who were living legends locally. Many of the last of the gas victims of the trenches of World War I were still resident in the nearby Leopardstown Hospital but sadly they too went un-interviewed. Another missed opportunity. I was learning, however slowly.

Did I teach with examinations always in mind? Hopefully not, but only pupils can really answer that question. If the curriculum demands were met, every opportunity was taken to introduce other important personalities from history. Ghandi, Roosevelt of the New Deal, even Robert Bruce was dragged in without mercy. The early days of teaching convinced me that the major problem was not 'intake' for pupils, but 'output' on paper. Inability to write essay-type and long paragraph questions was a serious concern addressed by the weekly class essay, which had to be written under exam conditions within the class. What was feared initially, within months became a pleasure for pupils, though it did add to the workload of corrections. These weekly 'press' deadlines were met as they trained themselves, not unlike greyhounds, to clock in impressive essays within thirty-seven minutes allotted.

They wrote to order as I sat reading the daily newspaper, counting down time in a loud menacing voice. Many of their efforts on paper, products of the clock tyranny, could have been published without editing in any daily newspaper. Scholars surpassed themselves and left me in their wake. I motivated, cajoled, pushed, encouraged and directed them to do what I never could, contradicting the Latin teaching maxim that you cannot give what you do not have yourself. This production line, once up and running, allowing for time constraints, never once sacrificed quality for quantity. The pupils vied with each other for weekly grades. They set their own standards. This was the essence of good teaching, which I accidentally stumbled on. What my boss or visiting teachers who called in from time to time, and who witnessed me reading the Sports column thought I was up to, embarrassed me only temporarily. I reminded myself that I was answerable only to those scribbling before me who were soaring high and free. Grounded as I was, their weekly essays were marked, admired and applauded.

History at senior level was not the most popular subject choice of pupils in the race for university points, and the resulting non-streamed mixed ability-classes posed serious questions for the teacher involved. Obviously all students were equally important. There could never be favourites. The high flyers I realised would progress and achieve with simple direction, all others needed to be taught. Motivation and praise were the staple diet. This overall teaching approach was pragmatic and open to regular review. When the right approach was stumbled upon one quickly forgot the numerous experiments that had failed. In time it more than proved itself when examinations came around. Like the Fates in the fables, the distinct threads of economics, culture, politics, religion, military and the much-neglected social history of people, which I labelled the Tom Dick, and Harry approach, were spun and stitched into the rich fabric of man's story. The long apprenticeship served in solitude, would have benefited greatly from the acquired wisdom of an older mentor, which sadly was not available. Assistance from any source would have been welcomed and made the journey easier. However, the question remains if my headstrong personality would have had the patience to listen.

In the classroom there were always wonderful lessons to be learned from pupils, none more important than it never paid to underestimate them. It is a blind teacher who fails to pick up signals from certain pupils who find the pace in class too fast and material uninteresting. For others too the watering down of the History topic under discussion in the hope of making it more palatable stretched patience if not credibility. My radar, ever active, registered such rumblings. Mixed ability classes imposed their own demand on the teacher. For the high-flyers I devised a signal system of my own to offset the boredom that prevented their forward march. The simple discreet finger tap on the desk when pacing up and down, was the green light indicating that they were free to unplug and study at a deeper level on their own quietly and undisturbed as I taught others, every bit as important, who needed pass grades. On such occasions the larger tomes of history books appeared from under the desks of pupils who were choosing from their own special á la carte menu that I never had the luxury or time to order from. Such pupils, voracious readers, set their own pace and accordingly appreciated the freedom given.

In the mid eighties, when pontificating at length on Socialism, I made a throwaway aside on Anarchism. Having read a lot of theory I was now professing to fully understand. My comment, innocently made, stung and rebounded in a wonderful manner. Stephen, red-faced and fuming, close neighbour and quiet as you were, I can still recall your reaction. You erupted and revolted in the best traditions of the subject under discussion and you threw down your own challenge to the existing status quo. 'Rubbish,' you voiced in a loud challenging tone, repeating it for those who were possibly slumbering or daydreaming at the time. 'Rubbish!' Was it perhaps the student barricades in Paris at the time that emboldened you? Now standing, you attacked saying I knew nothing about anarchism, adding that I was skating on thin ice, oblivious to the cracking noise under my feet. You were in full flight; you had come into your own. You were indeed correct in your assessment and there and then I yielded the floor, inviting you to educate us accordingly. What followed was a twenty-five minute lecture on Anarchism, Bakunin and Nihilism worthy of any university professor. You certainly put matters in a proper perspective and gave us food for thought much more sustaining and substantial than the meagre scraps I had brought to the table on that day. We applauded your scholarship and thanked you for setting matters straight. Though you rarely ever spoke again in the class you opened the door for many other scholarly pupils to enlighten us further, of which there was no shortage. I always bowed to superior knowledge at least from that moment out, and never felt threatened or upset when more learned heads contributed on topics they had researched and were obsessed with. One learned to tread softly in the knowledge that there were no real experts, only degrees of ignorance.

The years 1968-1998 were not always conducive to the teaching of Irish history. Big Brother, the eye of 'The Cruiser' at cabinet level and the media at different times surveyed the scene and spanceled the feet of many history teachers, mine included, from wandering into forbidden pastures. The troubles in the North loomed large; ballads banned went unsung, political voices were silenced and substituted in news reports, while pontificating revisionists redefined republicanism and nationalism. The daily violence, killings and bombings all were proof positive that sectarianism and militarism had once more raised their ugly heads. In the teaching of History I had restricted all wars including 1914-18; 1939-45 to causes and results. The dehumanising details involved in military campaigns were sufficiently reflected in film and T.V. without my adding to the appeal it had to young minds. The Cambodian killing fields, Vietnam's My Lai, Bloody Sunday, Shankill and Dublin bombings; like poisons the words hung in the air, making meaningful academic discussion at times impossible as passions were justifiably aroused. Like most of my generation sheltered from such traumas, the single shell-shocked veteran of my youth was a fading memory as were the Civil War participants. I cosseted my history classes from the horrors and glorification of war, and justified the stance when queried. Not all agreed, understandably, but I had only to answer to myself.

While my politics were a private matter, I resented the suspicion that a whole previous generation of idealistic teachers had to endure. Many of the Christian Brothers had unjustly been branded as republican firebrands in the decades after Independence. No allowance was made for the idealism of those who wished to be free of what they considered foreign shackles. The freedom of small nations somehow always seemed to exclude Ireland. Privately I railed against the suspicion that by implication History teachers of my generation had now to be kept in line, however subtle the insidious pressures. Ministerial pronouncements, newspaper editorials and letter columns, all were very effective pressures in themselves in silencing people. Republicanism, even with a small 'r', was a dangerous word to use, akin to membership of a Trade Union during the McCarthy period in the 1950's America. Teachers were in the front lines, an easy target. It may have been my sensitivities, but I felt unsure teaching on relatively recent Irish topics or in discussing events that were taking place sixty miles up the road, which cried out for attention. To argue in the staff room that the Bloody Sunday inquiry and the subsequent Widgery report was a whitewash was fine, but to debate the issue in a class of young men, even from a historic perspective, was a possible mine field. In later years the authorities encouraged and justified Sinn Féin's participation in northern coalitions yet decried it sixty miles further south. Such attitudes were difficult to understand; others still might call it a form of hypocrisy. Ignore the present, stay in the past. On a personal level it was difficult and upsetting. Ignoring it smacked of a type of intellectual arrogance. Discussion of those topics in class would have singled me out, left me open to criticism; no doubt other teachers felt threatened too. The elephant in the room was ignored. My token gesture to the Principal on the day of Sands' death mattered little; while refusing to teach I sat in silence in all classes, registering the point with my pupils. I now understand how young impressionable people got so caught up in the troubles in the North; it required very little to acknowledge the bugle in the blood. I was a fireside Republican who often ran for cover when matters got hot. I knew my limitations; the background of those years certainly cast a long shadow from which some teachers never emerged. If my mask fell on that one day, all through my teaching career I knew the heavy responsibility that I had as a history teacher. I would not abuse my position or influence others lest I too might have to ask the question that Yeats posed. I was well aware of how long it took the Civil War parties to dispose of the pike in the thatch!

'Did that play of mine
Send out
Certain young men the English shot?'

In the aftermath of the fiftieth anniversary of 1916 politicians quickly distanced themselves from the idealism that inspired it. I make no argument for the physical force tradition. I recoil from it. Conscious of objectivity I always pulled back from any worthwhile and wide-ranging debate on the Ulster Question which was relevant to our course, opting instead for the safe ground of Bismarck's long-forgotten foreign policy in the Balkans.

Yes, I funked the issue. Try discussing the North 1920-1950 without detailing gerrymandering, sectarianism, propaganda, or the Ulster mindset, not to mention the English Foreign Office and media stance. One must never forget that it was the English who mastered a language that could label Dunkirk a military triumph, rather than a resounding defeat. Too many truths had to be exposed before that would be possible. In partial compensation I discussed in detail and put on for house exams compulsory questions on all the worthwhile peace efforts, Sunningdale, referenda and elections. No parent objected. When evictions and burnings were at their height a weekly collection lasting over six months was taken up for a Falls Road family whose breadwinner was interred. To the credit of the De La Salle authorities, my employers, raised no objections, more aware than most of the difficulties on the ground in their own Belfast schools. The £10 weekly donation at the time was a princely sum. To balance the books, I wrote to the Rev. Ian forwarding a contribution of £50 in total, and to my eternal shame lost his generous letter of thanks in an office spring clean. Some history teachers should indeed be sent back to school! The more pressing issue of the hunger strike and the death of Bobby Sands affected me like nothing before. While direct comparisons may be strained, I was conscious of the role hunger strikes played in Irish history, especially by Cork's MacSwiney and McCurtain and later Ashe, all of whom reputedly inspired Ghandi.

The countdown of the Bobby Sands hunger strikes impacted on many;

it was a defining moment in history which sadly had to be ignored in class, in preference to the Versailles Treaty of 1919 or some other distant profound topic.

******

'I see from your C.V. you did History in school,' my Professor friend asked across the interview table in a major Dublin hospital. 'Yes,' came the nervous reply. 'I see.' 'Strictly from an observational point of view,' the professor continued, 'if your former teacher were to walk in that door behind you now, what is the first thought that would come into your head?' Like canons, the numbers 64/57 boomed back in reply, shattering the split-second silence. The professor, a close friend searching for a stick he could later use against me, now playing games, had set up the junior doctor and when the incident was related to me later in confidence, I took the reply as a high compliment. Better to be remembered for that than forgotten altogether. An explanation had to follow, naturally, as it will for most readers with the exception of a very select few who took part in the annual history class highlight, the 1922 Treaty Debate in Irish History. In preparation the events and personalities before the Civil War, Griffith, Pearse, Larkin, Connolly, 1916, were parsed and analysed, combed and sifted as no other topic throughout the year.

Our study always culminated in the Collins-De Valera split on the Treaty, which we re-enacted and voted anew. 'Volunteer' pupils, gang-pressed again, pitched the heated arguments of long ago from the class dais as the other anxious pupils and would-be voters listened, posing serious questions for our actors who on occasions dressed for the part. Dev and Collins again gave vent to their emotions, and were applauded accordingly. The whole exercise was worthwhile, informative and entertaining even when family loyalties and politics from home were reflected. Year after year I predicted the result on the back of a copybook as the class votes were cast in private, before the appointed tellers counted and announced the class result. The revisited treaty vote generally echoed the original percentage vote of Freestate 64 /Republican 57 as in 1923. That is until the hunger strike episode when the trend was reversed with a landslide result in favour of the Republican side. The lesson was not lost on me. Had I unconsciously on this one occasion been influenced by the turmoil in society and influenced my pupils in turn in my teaching that year? Pupils often queried my own political stance and views, and when they did I offered no enlightenment. The fact that I downed garden tools and presented myself in Merrion Square to witness, if not cheer, the burning of an Embassy, was not revealed. Neither was my special audience with President De Valera in the Áras days before he retired into civilian life. This was the written history page come to life. I kept my counsel but honestly admitted that as a result of the dramatic and forceful arguments by the opposing pupils year after year on numerous topics, I was often persuaded to switch from my original viewpoint and allegiance. However I regret to this day the missed opportunity to accompany a fellow teacher to witness the crumbling of the Berlin Wall.

I chuckle now on recalling the blunt class putdown directed at inquiring minds regarding the 'what if' questions in relation to specific historical events, e.g. 'What if Collins had survived the Civil War, Sir?' 'If Lenin had lived on, Sir?' Fuming, I contended that it was difficult enough to explain what did happen without speculating on what might have happened. In giving short shrift to the 'What if' school of historians little did I think that in the near future one of these chastened minds in a nearby class would confound and entertain the nation in his weekly radio programme 'What if'; I stand corrected and in admiration, and not for the first time either.

Yes, I did teach other subjects. 'Don't tell me you are still using those Buntús Cainte books, the red and blue Irish ones, Sir.' It was never a query, rather a rebuke for being old-fashioned and not keeping up with the educational trends. I always quipped back in the affirmative, and did so with confidence. The teaching of Irish in Dublin schools, often considered a tough task by others, I found easy. I did so initially at the highest-level Leaving Certificate, though the pupils put me to the pin of my collar to correct their impressive essays, as I had no Irish qualification in my degree. The standard of Irish in the feeder schools in the community varied considerably and consequently it dictated a flexible teaching approach in second level. Where problems existed, it some-times mirrored strong home beliefs calculated to undermine any child's motive to learn. 'What's the point in learning Irish?' was the oft-repeated dinner table chant. This dogmatic query was not easy to combat; it was a stumbling block that the younger minds could have well done without. More negative energy was wasted in the war of words and campaigns against so called compulsory Irish that would have, if channelled positively, fostered the language for generations to come.

I enjoyed teaching Irish and spoke it outside the school when the op-portunity arose, fully realising that my approach and methods were somewhat unusual and unorthodox in following the Buntús principle, for that was what I called it. The books in themselves, deceptively ef-fective, simplistic to the eye, had been based on a pioneering comput-erised study of the structure of Irish, illustrated in cartoon format in the early 1970's, incorporating drill patterns and informal grammar in three separate booklets over 180 short chapters. This presentation never failed to appeal to students who found the study of the language difficult. They laughed and at the same time the constant repetition and examples with explanatory English text allowed pupils teach themselves. Year after year these books worked for me where other ap-proaches failed. The result was positive, enjoyable learning and teach-ing. When I saw my own father, a scholar in his own right, reading from these booklets well into his retirement years, I knew I was on to a winner. Book 3 he admitted, if mastered, was the equivalent to a uni-versity degree in the language. For the record, they are available still in the Irish shop on the seafront in Bray. If they fail you, I could con-vince myself to give you a refund.

In following my own middle path between examinations and educa-tion, I often strayed and got lost. I refer specifically to prostituting my-self in cramming pupils for a separate extra Economic History paper in an effort to gain double points, just like maths enjoyed over years for University entry. A one-day crash course with the occasional after-school class prepared pupils sufficiently to sit this extra exam. When pupils gained entry to eagerly sought courses with the double points,

I somehow justify my actions, but it was not education, and I am not proud to admit to cramming and grinding. This was situation ethics in operation at its best. Such was the daily routine of my life in the classroom. Given the opportunity I would gladly repeat it all over again.

IN CONCLUSION

Does the recent paper entitled 'Changing society, Changing schools,' from the hierarchy who are in effect patrons of eighty per cent of all schools in Ireland, herald change and hope, as it envisages teachers playing a much greater role counselling in the future? Many of the younger generation are, it has to be accepted, now alienated from the traditional and religious moral forces that influenced their parents. Will they seek direction, however short-term, from teachers who will be looked upon not just as academic instructors but publicists of the much needed moral and ethical code required for the smooth running of a changed society? Is this new paper an early sign of the vote of confidence that I have been expecting? If so, it is welcomed. As a retired teacher I will have no part to play in this proposed new role, but on second thoughts, I may after all have been unconsciously fulfilling such a role in these time-out classes, which I considered more important than any of my academic work. They certainly were more relevant. Can I now take this as a retrospective sanction, even approval, for what was attempted in those reality briefings? The plurality of school patronage will change in the new Ireland and accordingly the role and influence the teacher once had in society might be regained, which may allow him to again make a more important contribution in an expanding multi-racial society. As a professional body, teachers have not been found wanting in the past and neither one hopes will they be in the future.

I like to think my classes were entertaining, if unpredictable. Exams had their place, they were important, but they were not to be confused with education. In themselves, they were possibly a tyranny and straitjacket for all concerned. The treadmill had to be negotiated and at times it dehumanised our efforts, as the utilitarian argument, the points system for university, the curse of the modern system made its own demands.

To the surprise of many teachers and the Principal I made a strong request to be allowed the opportunity to teach my own son when he entered the school. For five years he too became my pupil. Why, you may ask? Simply on the grounds that if I was good enough to teach other people's children, the least I could do was teach my own son. Some may consider such action a recipe for disaster, but in reality it posed no problem for me, or for him, as he admitted years later. He was another pupil no more or no less than the others in the seats before me. Above all I wished him to see me as others saw me, not just as a cranky father, but also as a teacher who tried hard, warts and all. Suffice to say that we both survived and benefited. Never once did I regret the privilege I was afforded. It was an enriching experience all round, possibly the highlight of the decades I spent in teaching. To have chosen otherwise would have left questions like 'What if,' not to mention the fact that it would have been an easy 'cop out' which I would have regretted forever.

When tired, frustrated or simply bored with the grind of classroom routine I always knew that a short visit to the Art department would instantly recharge low batteries. Through the good offices of a succession of teachers, latterly Tim, I was welcomed in possibly because I ignored their best efforts to keep me out. My abiding interest was no doubt a vain attempt to make up for the deficiency in my own education, which neglected art appreciation and the visual arts. Full of admiration of the freedom and work produced, I was also envious of the opportunity afforded those pupils and denied to me. The fifteen paintings by pupils, all commissioned and paid for, that adorn the various walls of my home is proof solid of my obsession with art. Each in turn speaks to me and is treasured. I was a patron of sorts, realising that the paintings I commissioned boosted the self-confidence and gave bragging rights to budding aspiring artists. Foolishly I had convinced myself that now with my eye educated some of the talent might rub off on me over time. Who could blame me? Did I not promise in retirement to reward myself and fulfil a lifetime's ambition and paint, once the decks were cleared? A promise not forgotten, just postponed, as a recent Mayo weekend tuition has re-ignited and whetted the appetite anew. If the artistic calligraphy of Denis Brown absorbs me, the works of Mark, Shane, Cormac, Philip, Garret and cartoonist John are equally treasured as daily reminders of those weekly excursions into their studio. Each in turn proved to be artistic, but then they learned from a good master. In the coming days, were I only to daub paint on canvas with my fingers the pleasure in doing so would be a sufficient reward in itself. I can only agree with the quotation of A.K. Coomaraswamy on the Art Room door, 'An artist is not a special type of man, but every man is a special type of artist.'

It would be easy to claim that in my final years I was teaching on autopilot. Nothing was further from the truth. Each new day taught me a new lesson. Each new pupil forced me to view matters in a new light and none more so than the pupil in the following brief story.

Knock. Knock. Office Door.

'Come in. Not you again. What's up now?'
 'I'm here to collect a detention form.'
'Are you trying to set a record? How many is this now?'
 'Just two in the last month, Sir.'
'Sit down there and let's get to the bottom of all this constant messing. Are you being bullied in the yard?'
 'Me, Sir? You must be joking.'
'Is some teacher getting at you?'
 'No, Sir.'
'Can you keep up with the class work?'
 'Yes Sir, when I study.'
'Yes Sir, No Sir, this is getting us nowhere. Is there anything you want to talk about? Well?'

(Long silence. Head shake.)

 'No, Sir.'
'Here's your bloody form so. Clear off to class, and before you go take a good look at that door ... it's always open. Remember that. If you want to talk, feel free to come in. It's not as if we don't see enough of each other, however maybe.............'

'Yes, Sir.'
'In spite of what you think, I can listen too.'
'I'll go back to class so, Sir.'
'Fine.'

Year Master's office – a phone call, one week later.

'Am I talking to the Year Master?'
'Yes.'
'Good. You were talking to my son last week (identifying himself).'
'A one-sided conversation if I might say so.'
'Not surprising.'
'He doesn't say much, does he?'
'Only when he has to. Can I share a confidentiality with you? Remember now I never phoned, just in case he asks.'
'I understand totally.'
'His mother, my wife has only a few weeks left. Terminal cancer.'
'I'm so sorry. I never knew.'
'Nobody knows. We're fine. As a family we had our round-table conference three months ago. We are coping well, all things considered.'
'How's he taking it?'
' To be truthful, he's incredible, but I want you to keep an eye on him. He's nearly a better cook and housekeeper than his mother, and he only fifteen. Runs the whole house, and shopping etc. My wife and I are very proud of him.'
'You must be.'
'Late at night and early every morning he creeps in to her room and lies down in the bed beside her, sometimes for an hour. All I hear is giggling and laughter. I think I am missing out on something. No mother and son were ever closer. What did he say to me last night?'
'Please tell me.'
'Dad, you must prepare to let Ma go, just like me. We are lucky to have had the months to say goodbye. He keeps me going. Where he gets his strength from I'll never know.'
'I'm sorry for your troubles.'
'You will keep an eye on him?'
'Of course, I promise.'
'Thank you.'

I would like to claim credit for some part in this story, but I cannot, as I never taught the pupil in question. On the funeral day I visited the house only to be greeted warmly by the pupil himself. For him death, untimely and sad, had been faced down. Maturity beyond his years. Who was the teacher and who was the pupil now? In relaying this story I am not breaking any confidence as the father in question approves of my doing so in the hope that it will, as it must surely, assist other teenagers in similar circumstances. And to think that in our relationship with him all the time we as teachers were distracted and zoning in on school trivialities. Step forward, young man. I stand in admiration. You taught us all a lesson, a lesson that will last.

Reluctantly I withdraw now, closing the door gently on the rich memories of a lifetime spent teaching. Yes there was deep satisfaction, enjoyment and friendship that no doubt will sustain me in the days ahead. I travelled my own road, but never alone. I liked to think of myself as a benign dictator with a human side, mischievous even a little eccentric, who over the years was forced to reassess methods and strategies in the best interests of pupils. This to me was the cutting edge, an uncomfortable position in itself, like the handling of a sharp blade.

Now that I am retired I miss the contact with young vibrant teenagers, the daily cut and thrust, the rapport, not to mention friendship, more than I ever expected. I always thought, as the words of the song put it, that 'there were more songs in me than would be sung.' But time is the master. When the curtain falls the stage must be vacated as others remain in the wings eagerly awaiting and deserving of their turn. I had finally trained myself to leave the classroom when the bell rang!

POSTSCRIPT

If my intention in writing a memoir was to evict and silence the countless individuals who still peopled my brain in retirement, I now readily admit that I have failed gloriously.

Since launching Mr. Mac, thanks in no small part to the power of the internet, a tsunami of long-gone pupils, scattered worldwide, has deluged me. This private publication has resulted in renewed contact, updated me and finally answered many questions about the whereabouts of those who are recalled as teenagers. Their unexpected and welcomed re-entry into my life has been a most rewarding experience and is proof positive that a reservoir of goodwill exists for teachers in general. It is important that this is appreciated by a profession who in today's economic climate find themselves in the glare of the media spotlight that often misrepresents honest efforts made, but hopefully too in the expectation that the education system might again play the important role that it did in times past.

This memoir was a quest, an eccentric private and interior quest with the added challenge of giving significance to the life of a teacher where nothing much appears to happen. The possibility that the story might be of interest to other young teachers starting out was encouraging and has, in truth, been a surprising bonus.

Communicating with adult former pupils goes beyond nostalgia as on occasions bridges have to be repaired on both sides. Many have scaled dizzy heights since they left, found fulfilment, and continue with the daily struggles in life. On hearing their stories I envy them their experiences, and welcome their deep-seated desire to renew acquaintance with far-flung classmates, some of whom are sadly no longer with us but are still fondly remembered by all their friends.

I trust that as a result of my initiative other teachers might be encouraged to write about their teaching lives, and experience how rewarding the journey can be. It certainly has put a smile on my face!

- Rud éigin déanta -

Cover design and layout by Design at DBA
Printed in Ireland by Gemini International Ltd.